MW00873910

THE GIANT

BOOK OF GAMES

FOR CHILDREN'S MINISTRY

Group

Loveland, Colorado
group.com

Group resources really work!

This Group resource incorporates our R.E.A.L. approach to ministry. It reinforces a growing friendship with Jesus, encourages long-term learning, and results in life transformation, because it's

Relational
Learner-to-learner interaction enhances learning and builds Christian friendships.

Experiential
What learners experience through discussion and action sticks with them up to 9 times longer than what they simply hear or read.

Applicable
The aim of Christian education is to equip learners to be both hearers and doers of God's Word.

Learner-based
Learners understand and retain more when the learning process takes into consideration how they learn best.

The Giant Book of Games for Children's Ministry

Copyright © 2013 Group Publishing, Inc.

All rights reserved. No part of this book may be reproduced in any manner whatsoever without prior written permission from the publisher, except where noted in the text and in the case of brief quotations embodied in critical articles and reviews. For information, visit group.com/permissions.

Visit our website: group.com

CREDITS
Chief Creative Officer: Joani Schultz
Executive Editor: Christine Yount Jones
Editor: Jennifer Hooks
Compiling Editors: David Jennings and Stephanie Martin
Copy Editor: Erica L. Feucht
Cover Art Director: Sheila Reinhardt
Cover Illustrator: Chris Boyd
Interior Designer: Jean Bruns
Production Artist: Pamela Poll/Pamela Poll Design
Interior Illustrator: Patrick Girouard/Portfolio Solutions, LLC

Unless otherwise indicated, all Scripture quotations are taken from the *Holy Bible* New Living Translation, copyright © 1996, 2004, 2007. Used by permission of Tyndale House Publishers, Inc. Carol Stream, Illinois 60188. All rights reserved.

ISBN 978-1-4707-0424-7

10 9 8 7 6 5 4 3 2 1   19 18 17 16 15 14 13

Printed in the United States of America.

Contents

· ·

Preschool Games

· ·

Early Elementary Games

GIANT BOOK OF GAMES FOR CHILDREN'S MINISTRY

Upper Elementary Games

Indexes

Introduction

Games go with childhood. And they go with your children's ministry, too! When kids are playing, they're learning. They're building relationships, making discoveries, and challenging themselves physically and mentally. Games are great growth stimulators—especially when it's faith you're trying to grow!

Kids from preschoolers to preteens need play as a regular part of their daily developmental diet. If you're spiritually nourishing kids, you need this book in your back pocket. Each of the 200+ games in this book is specifically designed to deepen kids' understanding of a Bible point or concept while evoking emotion through fun and unexpected experiences. Kids will find real-life meaning in the midst of laughter and play, and they'll experience Scripture in new and memorable ways.

When kids have fun in your ministry, they want to come back. The games in this book add fun to every moment you have with them. So go ahead and start thumbing through—you'll find hundreds of games that teach kids compassion, faithfulness, gratitude, forgiveness, grace, and so much more—all while solidifying biblical learning.

In your hands you hold the perfect complement to every lesson, event, or extra five minutes you have with kids. Are you ready?

Get Set, Go!

Here's a snapshot of the different ways you can use this book to find the game you need.

TOPIC

Each game is categorized by topic. If you're looking for a specific lesson or topic, simply scan the topics in the Topic Index on page 246.

SCRIPTURE

Many games have a direct Scripture link. To find a game based on a Scripture, just go the Scripture Index on page 243.

GAME OVERVIEW

Each game provides an at-a-glance overview. This summary gives you the underlying message of the game in one sentence.

ENERGY LEVEL

Each game is categorized as Low, Medium, or High Energy Level to help you plan ahead with accurate expectations for each game. To find a game based on Energy Level, just go to the Energy Level Index on page 240.

SUPPLY LEVEL

Each game is rated as Low, Medium, or High Supply Level to best fit your needs. Games requiring between 1 and 2 supply categories are rated Low Supply Level games. Medium Supply Level games will require between 3 and 4 supply categories, and High Supply Level games call for 5+ supply categories. To find a game based on Supply Level, just go to the Supply Level Index on page 250.

AGE LEVEL

All games are categorized according to the age levels they work best with: 3 to 5; 6 to 9; and 10 to 12. The book reflects these three sections for quick look-up. Some games work with multiple age groups, reflected in the Age Level rating at the beginning of each game.

Safety First!

MAGNET WARNING

MAGNET WARNING! For activities with magnets, use only large magnets that can't be swallowed, and warn kids against putting a magnet anywhere near their face. A swallowed magnet is a medical emergency, so take steps to discourage kids from doing anything but the assignment with the magnets, and collect them when the activity is over.

BALLOON WARNING

BALLOON WARNING! Children under 8 years of age can choke or suffocate on uninflated or broken balloons. Adult supervision required. Keep uninflated balloons from children. Discard broken balloons at once. Balloons may contain latex.

ALLERGY ALERTS

ALLERGY ALERT! Be aware that some kids have allergies to certain foods and other materials. The games in this book that include these items have an Allergy Alert symbol. Always check with parents to see whether children have allergies or dietary concerns beforehand.

The Giant Book of Games provides numerous ways to quickly find the game you need. You'll find comprehensive indexes for Energy Level, Scripture, Topic, and Supply Level.

Enjoy!

Preschool
GAMES

It's true: All kids love games! But preschoolers especially love them!

Little ones delight in game-based play in a carefree, joyous way that's unique to their age group. And kids this age learn best when they engage in play and games.

Every game in this section is designed specifically for kids ages 3 to 5. You'll find noncompetitive, faith-focused games that teach preschoolers a Bible point, and can be used in almost any setting. You'll find Scripture references to prompt little ones to begin looking at the Bible as well as discussion questions that boost kids' understanding of what they're learning and experiencing.

Let's play!

Best for

AGES 3-5

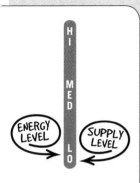

SCRIPTURE
Psalm 91:11-12

SUPPLIES
Bible, feathers

PREPARATION
none

Angel Wings

Kids get to be brushed by "angel wings."

Show kids how to lightly brush another child's forearm with a feather, and say: **Let's pretend this is what it feels like to be brushed by an angel's wing.**

Choose one-fourth to one-third of the kids to be "Angels," and have them stand at the front of the room. Give each Angel a feather.

Have the other kids lie facedown on the floor with their eyes closed and their faces hidden in the crook of their elbows.

Ask each Angel to quietly walk through the room and lightly brush a different child's forearm and then return to the front of the room and put down their feathers.

When the Angels return to the front of the room, have the other children sit up. If an Angel's wing brushed them, they can stand. Call on these kids to identify who they think brushed them. Once kids have guessed, they get to trade places with the Angel who brushed them.

Play until everyone's been brushed by an Angel's wing or until everyone's had a chance to be an Angel.

Debrief

At the end of the game, discuss the following.

- *What was it like to be brushed by an Angel's wing?*
- *What do you think angels do?*
- *In what ways do you think God's angels help us?*

Read aloud Psalm 91:11-12.

Say: **God sends angels to watch out for us. Even though we can't see them, they're "brushing" by us every day, protecting us.**

Close in prayer, thanking God for angels to keep us safe.

AGES 3-5

Esther Wrap

Kids race to see what it's like to be "queen."

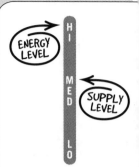

SCRIPTURE

Esther 2:17-18

SUPPLIES

Bible, markers, toilet paper, bag of treats per group of four

PREPARATION

ALLERGY ALERT!
See page 8

Read aloud Esther 2:17-18.

Say: **The king really loved Esther. He was very kind to her like she was very kind to others. He gave her a beautiful crown and threw a big party for her. She got to wear beautiful clothing and priceless jewels. Let's play a game to imagine being Esther for a moment!**

Form teams of no more than four. Set the toilet paper, markers, and bags of candy in the center of your room. Have kids choose one person on their team who'll be "Esther."

Say: **On "Go!" your group will race to make a toilet paper crown and shawl for your Queen Esther using toilet paper and markers. As soon as Esther's crown and shawl are done, you'll sit on the floor around Esther's feet. Ready, go!**

When all the groups are done, say: **Great job! Now, the Esthers from each group can come to the center of the room and choose a bag of treats. Then take it back to your group and serve them to say "thank you" for making you look so wonderful!**

Allow time, and encourage kids to enjoy their treats.

Debrief

Afterward, discuss the following.

- *What was this game like for you?*
- *What was it like to be Esther?*
- *What was it like to have Esther serve you a treat?*

Say: **Esther lived in a place where people didn't worship God. But God worked through her to help his people. God wants us to help and serve one another whenever we can.**

AGES 3-5

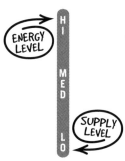

2 Corinthians 13:11

Bible

Group Tag

Kids discover how having good friends makes life better.

Say: **Let's play a game that shows it's important to encourage each other.**

Choose one child to be "It." Have It chase the other children and try to catch them. When It catches someone, It has to say something nice or encouraging to the child to keep him or her.

Once It says something nice, the caught child joins hands with It, and they both try to catch others. The person who catches a child is the one to say something nice to the child he or she catches.

Stop play when everyone is holding hands.

Debrief

At the end of the game, discuss the following.

- *What was it like to catch friends with nice words?*
- *How can encouraging each other make life better?*
- *Why do you think God wants us to encourage each other?*

Read aloud 2 Corinthians 13:11. Say: **This verse tells us to encourage each other. When we're nice and encourage each other, it makes life a lot more fun.**

AGES 3-5

Friendship Fishing

Children go "fishing" for good friends.

Have kids form two groups, and give each child a piece of construction paper and a marker. Show everyone how to tear out two fish shapes from the paper. Direct one group to think about words that describe good friends and help kids write those words on their fish and draw a happy face. Ask the other group to do the same with words that describe someone who's not such a good friend and draw a frowning face.

Distribute paper clips. Help kids slide a paper clip onto the tail of their fish and place them on the bedsheet "sea" with the printed side up. Have kids sit around the sea.

Say: **We all enjoy having friends, but God wants us to choose friends who care for us. True friends make our lives more fun and enjoyable.**

Read aloud Proverbs 18:24.

Say: **This verse means that we need to carefully choose our friends, and that true friends are like family.**

Say: **Let's go fishing for friends. We'll take turns using this pretend fishing pole. Keep any fish that has the characteristic of a true friend with a happy face. Throw the other fish back into the sea.**

Have kids fish for friends. Make sure everyone gets to catch a keeper.

 SCRIPTURE

Proverbs 18:24

 SUPPLIES

Bible, construction paper, markers, metal paper clips, bedsheet, magnet, string, yardstick

 **PREPARATION**

Attach a magnet to the end of a 2-foot piece of string. Tie the other end of the string onto the end of the yardstick.

MAGNET WARNING!
See page 8

Debrief

Afterward, ask everyone:

- *What was easy or difficult about this game?*
- *How can you find good friends?*
- *How can you be a good friend?*

Say: **God made us so we could have friends. We may have lots of friends or a few, but we can choose friends who make our hearts happy.**

Best for

AGES 3-5

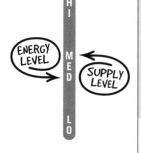

Trusting God

Kids hunt for items and learn about God's provision.

SCRIPTURE

Luke 12:22-24

SUPPLIES

Bible; timer or stopwatch; winter clothes such as coats, sweaters, gloves, scarves, and so on (enough so each child will have at least one item to wear)

PREPARATION

Before children arrive, hide the winter clothes throughout your room.

Say: **God gives us what we need. Let's pretend it's very cold and we will learn about what God gives us.** Have kids close their eyes and imagine it's frigid and they're very cold and shivering. **All around this room I've hidden things God has given us to get warm. But you have to look for the items, and you only have one minute.**

Then let kids hunt for hidden coats, sweaters, gloves, and other winter wear. After time is up and kids have found the clothing, have them put on the clothes. Then read aloud Luke 12:22-24, focusing on how God provides for our needs.

Debrief

After the game, discuss the following.

- *Tell about one thing you need every day and why you need it.*
- *What does God give you to help with that need?*

Say: **Just like we were able to find the winter items to keep us warm, God provides for our needs.** As children take off the winter clothes, take turns with kids discussing ways God has met their needs.

Best for

AGES 3-5

Telephone

Children remember to listen carefully when a message is important.

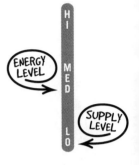

ENERGY LEVEL

HI
MED
LO

SUPPLY LEVEL

✝ SCRIPTURE

Matthew 7:28-29

🛍 SUPPLIES

Bible

☑ PREPARATION

Think of some tongue-twister sentences.

Have kids sit in a circle. If you have more than 10 kids, form more than one circle. Read aloud Matthew 7:28-29, and then say: **When Jesus talks to me, I want to listen to every word he says!**

But sometimes it's hard to keep a message straight. Let's try something. I'll whisper one sentence in the ear of the person on my right. That person will whisper it to the person on his or her right, and so on around the circle. Try to repeat the sentence the same way you heard it. While you're not listening or whispering, chant this with me:

*I listen when I'm sitting,
I listen when I'm walking.
Except that I can't listen—
When I'm too busy talking!*

Start the chant, and then whisper to the person on your right: **Which way went the window washer?** When the message makes it around the circle back to you, repeat what was said. It may be the same—but it probably won't be.

Play a few rounds, then start sentences going *both* directions around the circle. Make up your own sentences, and keep the chant going.

Debrief

After you repeat what you heard, ask:

- *What made it difficult to listen?*
- *What makes it difficult to listen to God sometimes?*
- *What can we do to listen to God better?*

AGES 3-5

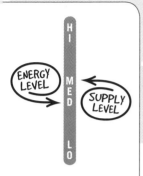

Happy Harvesters

Kids remember to be thankful for all that God has given them.

SUPPLIES

one toy fruit or vegetable for each pair of children; one sturdy, disposable plate per child

PREPARATION

TIP Give kids "less round" toy fruits, such as bananas or bunches of grapes or cherries—these are easier to manage.

Help children form pairs. Have kids form two lines in the middle of the room with partners facing each other, about an arm's length apart. Ensure there's plenty of space, so kids can step farther apart as they play.

Give each child a sturdy, disposable plate. Place a toy fruit or vegetable on each plate in one line. One child from each pair will have a fruit or vegetable. Say: **Hold your plates with both hands and toss the fruit or vegetable to your partner using only the plate. Try to catch the food on your plates as you toss it back and forth.** Have pairs practice.

Now that you've got that down, let's try this. After you catch it, take one small step backward. If you drop the fruit or vegetable, scoop it up with the plate, and name one thing you're thankful for before tossing it again.

Let kids bend their plates slightly to make it easier to keep the fruit or vegetable on the plate.

Debrief

After the game gather kids in a circle, discuss the following.

• *What's something you're thankful for?*
• *How does God help us every day?*
• *How can we show God we're thankful?*

Say: **We can give thanks to God for everything every single day.**

Tell kids you're going to thank God now. Start the prayer by holding a toy fruit. Say: **"Thank you God, for** [something you're thankful for]**."** Then pass the item to the child next to you, who'll name something and then toss the item to the next child, and so on until everyone has had a turn.

Everyone's Invited

AGES 3-5

Kids learn that God's gift to us is eternal life.

Have kids sit in a circle.

Say: **We're going to pass the beanbag around the circle like we do when we play the game Hot Potato. If you get the beanbag, act like it's really hot and pass it to someone else quickly. Let's practice that.** Allow time for kids to practice.

Say: **Now let's play. When I say "Stop!" the person holding the beanbag gets to stand up and walk to the corner called "Heaven." Show kids the sign. Play the game until four kids are in Heaven, and announce that the game is over.**

 Debrief

At the end of the game, discuss the following.

- *What was it like to get the beanbag?*
- *What was it like not to get the beanbag?*

Say: **Let's play again.** This time, play until everyone is in heaven.

After the game, ask:

- *What do you hope heaven is like?*
- *Why do you think God wants us all in heaven with him?*

Read aloud John 10:27-29. Say: **Eternal life lasts forever in heaven with God. According to these verses, how do we get to heaven?**

Say: **When we believe in Jesus, we'll live with him forever in heaven. We can tell others that good news, so they'll be in heaven with us, too!**

 SCRIPTURE

John 10:27-29

SUPPLIES

Bible, beanbag or rolled up sock, poster board or butcher paper, marker

 **PREPARATION**

Using the butcher paper or poster board and marker, make a sign that says "Heaven" and place it in one corner of your room.

Best for

AGES 3-5

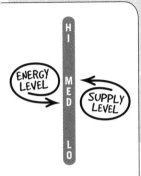
ENERGY LEVEL

SUPPLY LEVEL

Friendship Fun

Kids explore ways to love one another.

SCRIPTURE

Luke 6:27-31

SUPPLIES

Bible, bubble wands, and containers of bubble solution

PREPARATION

TIP This game is best played with older preschoolers.

Open your Bible to Luke 6:27-31, and briefly summarize what Jesus taught about loving enemies. Then read aloud Luke 6:31.

Say: **Jesus wants us to love others and treat them like we'd like to be treated. Let's play a game to help us remember that.**

Have kids form pairs, and give each pair a container of bubble solution and a bubble wand. Explain that partners are going to take turns telling each other about a time someone hurt their feelings.

The first child will tell about an experience with hurt feelings and then blow a bubble. The other child will pop the bubble and then tell one way to forgive the person who hurt his or her feelings and treat that person as Jesus said. Have kids switch roles after each turn.

Debrief

When everyone has had a few turns, gather everyone together. Ask:

- *Why is it hard to love people who hurt your feelings?*
- *Why do you think God wants you to love everyone, even people who hurt your feelings?*
- *What are ways you heard that you can show love to others?*

AGES 3-5

How Long?

Kids work to see how long they can be perfect at something.

SUPPLIES

pencils

PREPARATION

Say: **Let's all stand on one foot to see who can do it the longest. Try to stand perfectly still! As soon as your other foot touches the ground, sit on the floor.** When everyone is down, start over. Allow some time for everyone to try this activity one or two times. Then give a pencil to each child.

Say: **Point three fingers of the same hand toward me, and keep them touching. Now try to balance the pencil perfectly across the back of your three fingers. See how long you can balance it. As soon as it falls, sit on the floor.** Give kids a few moments to practice, and then have them try to balance the pencils. Collect the pencils and have everyone sit.

Say: **Now let's see how long you can sit perfectly still without even one little wiggle. Is everyone ready? Go!** Wait until one or two children wiggle.

Say: **Sometimes trying to be good all the time is like the games we just played. We can do it for a little while, but then we mess up.**

Debrief

At the end of the game, discuss the following.

- *What were you thinking when you were trying to be perfect in this game? after you messed up?*
- *Why can't we be perfect all the time?*
- *Why do you think God still loves us even when we're not perfect all the time?*

Say: **As hard as we try, we'll never be good all the time. But there's someone who is—Jesus. Jesus never sinned! That's amazing because we know how hard it is to be good all the time. Let's jump and clap to tell Jesus we think he's awesome!**

Best for

AGES 3-5

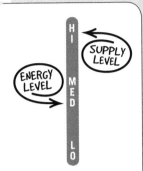

SCRIPTURE

John 3:16-17

SUPPLIES

Bible, colorful
construction paper, black
marker, tape, praise
music, music player

PREPARATION

Tape a variety of colors
of construction paper
pieces in a random
pattern on the floor,
ensuring there are four
or five pieces per child.
Prepare to play praise
music.

Rescued

Kids discover that Jesus
is our rescuer.

Say: **Let's play a game. Everyone, find a piece of construction paper to stand on. Let's pretend that the papers on the floor are stepping stones over a raging river. You have to stay on the papers, or hungry crocodiles will eat you! Walk around the room while I play the music. When the music stops, stand still on one paper.**

Play music for a few seconds, and then stop it.

Say: **Oh no! The crocodiles have swallowed all the** [name a color of construction paper] **stepping stones. If you're on a** [same color of construction paper] **stepping stone, move to another color quickly!**

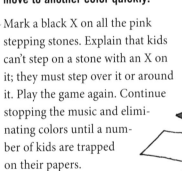

Mark a black X on all the pink stepping stones. Explain that kids can't step on a stone with an X on it; they must step over it or around it. Play the game again. Continue stopping the music and eliminating colors until a number of kids are trapped on their papers.

Say: **Uh-oh. It looks like some of you are trapped. You need a rescuer. I'm a rescuer. If you hold my hand, you'll be saved from the hungry crocodiles.**

Escort kids out of "danger" one by one. If there are still quite a few children who aren't trapped, continue playing. When most of the children are trapped and rescued, end the game.

Say: **We get trapped by the wrong things we do. The Bible tells us that Jesus is our rescuer.**

Read aloud John 3:16-17.

• • (Debrief) • •

At the end of the game, discuss the following.

- *What were you thinking when you were trapped?*
- *Tell about a time you got in trouble for doing something wrong.*
- *What was it like to have someone rescue you?*

Say: **Getting in trouble feels a little bit like being trapped. When we do wrong things, we feel bad. But Jesus can rescue us by forgiving us. God sent Jesus to save us from the wrong things we do because God loves us so much.**

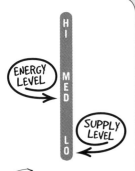

AGES 3-5

Prayer Webs

Kids build prayer webs of support for each other.

SCRIPTURE

Galatians 6:2-3

SUPPLIES

Bible, small ball (a soccer ball works great)

PREPARATION

Say: **Let's make a web. Here's how we'll do it. Stand shoulder-to-shoulder in two lines facing each other. Cross your left arm over your right arm and grab the hands of the person across from you.** If you have an uneven number of kids, have an adult volunteer join in so everyone has a partner.

When kids have done this, say: **Now I'm going to toss this ball onto your web. Let's see if you can support it.**

Toss the ball onto the children's arms. Encourage them not to drop the ball.

Say: **Now let's see if you can pass the ball from one end of the line to the other and back.**

Then have kids work together to pass the ball to each other.

After a few minutes of play, say: **You wouldn't have been able to accomplish this task if you hadn't worked together. Let's see what God's Word has to say about working together.**

Read aloud Galatians 6:2-3.

Say: **One way God wants us to work together and support each other is by praying for others, just like the web of hands we created together today helped us keep the ball going.**

Debrief

At the end of the game, discuss the following.

- *Why do you think it helps our friends when we pray for them?*
- *What are things you can pray for to help your friends and family?*

End by asking willing children to pray for the group (go ahead and pray if kids are reluctant to do so). Encourage kids to continue praying for each other throughout the week.

Helping Others

A Gentle Game

Kids explore how to be gentle servants by following Jesus' example.

AGES 3-5

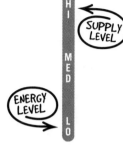

SUPPLY LEVEL

ENERGY LEVEL

Give each child a packing peanut or a cotton ball. Provide markers and encourage children to mark their peanut so they'll recognize it. (You may need to help younger children with this.)

Say: **Often when people talk about Jesus being a servant, they call him a gentle servant.**

Read aloud John 13:1-5.

Say: **Jesus was gentle and loving. We're going to practice being gentle. Everyone put your packing peanut on the floor.**

Point out the dustpans around the room and say: **Your goal is to get your peanut into a dustpan, but you can't touch the packing peanut. You can blow on it or fan it with a piece of paper to try to get it where you want it to be. Be gentle.** Offer paper for kids who want to try fanning their packing peanuts into a dustpan.

Let kids blow and fan their peanuts until they get them into one of the dustpans. They can help each other as long as they're gentle.

SCRIPTURE

John 13:1-5

SUPPLIES

Bible, dustpans, non-dissolving foam packing peanuts or cotton balls, markers, paper

PREPARATION

Set several dustpans around the room.

TIP Some packing peanuts dissolve in water. Be sure to use waterproof packing peanuts.

 Debrief

After the game, discuss:

- *Explain what it was like to be gentle.*
- *How was Jesus gentle with his friends?*
- *How can you serve someone else this week?*

Say: **Jesus wouldn't mind washing your hands or helping you blow your nose or fixing you a snack. The time Jesus washed the disciples' feet helps us understand that to be like Jesus, we must be gentle and willing to serve our friends.**

Best for

AGES 3-5

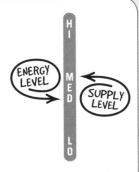
ENERGY LEVEL

SUPPLY LEVEL

H
I
M
E
D
L
O

Luke 6:46-49

SUPPLIES

Bible; masking tape; one piece of each: red, yellow, and green construction paper

PREPARATION

Using the masking tape, create three 6' x 6' boxes side by side on the floor. In the center of each box, tape down one piece of paper, with the yellow one in the middle box.

Traffic Jam

Kids play a game about obeying to remind them to do what Jesus says.

Read aloud Luke 6:46-49

Say: **Jesus said that if we don't obey, our lives could end up in a big mess. Let's play a game to remind us of that. The three colors in the boxes represent the colors of a traffic light.**

Remind younger kids what the colors of a traffic light indicate. Have everyone stand in the yellow (middle) square. Say: **When I shout out another color, move quickly to the appropriate square.**

If you have older kids, you can make the game more challenging by occasionally calling out the color of the square where kids are already standing. For older kids, anyone who steps out of the square is out until he or she performs a simple task such as jumping jacks or counting to 10.

Say: **For a change of pace, if I call out "Traffic jam!" everyone must step outside all of the squares.**

Keep the pace fast, and vary the colors. Continue play as time allows. Then have kids sit together in the squares.

Debrief

Discuss the following.

- *In this game, you had to listen carefully and follow all the directions. What was it like to try to obey my signals?*
- *What kinds of things does Jesus tell us to do?*
- *Why do you think it's important to follow what Jesus says?*

Say: **Jesus tells us what to do because he loves us and knows what's best for us. Jesus always gives us good instructions to follow, and we can always trust him.**

Best for

AGES 3-5

Fire Walker

Kids explore the courage of Shadrach, Meshach, and Abednego in the fiery furnace.

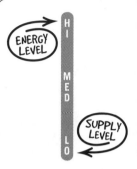

SCRIPTURE

Daniel 3

SUPPLIES

Bible

PREPARATION

Open your Bible to Daniel 3, and summarize what happened to Shadrach, Meshach, and Abednego. Then form two groups. Have one group scatter around the middle of the room and sit down at least an arm's length apart. Direct the other group to stand against one wall.

Say: **In this passage, we learn of three men who were thrown into a huge fire because they wouldn't worship a golden statue. Let's pretend that this group of kids in the middle is a group of "Flames."**

Flames, your job is to try to reach out and try to touch the kids walking through. Have the Flames raise their hands and wiggle their fingers. They may want to make crackling and hissing noises as well.

Say: **Now let's see if the other group can carefully walk through the fire to the other wall without getting "burned"—or touched by a Flame. You'll have to be brave, like Shadrach, Meshach, and Abednego! If one of the Flames touches you, sit down and join the Flames and try to touch others who are walking through.**

Give a signal, and have kids start walking through the fire. Encourage the kids who reach the opposite wall to walk back without getting touched. Encourage all kids to imagine how Shadrach, Meshach, and Abednego trusted God to keep them safe from the real flames.

Play until one child is left. Then have the groups switch roles and play again.

Debrief

At the end of the game, discuss the following.

- *What did you do that was brave during this game?*
- *How did the three men in the Bible show courage?*
- *What can you do to show that you trust God when you're afraid?*

TOPIC

Creation

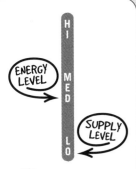

Best for

AGES 3-5

ENERGY LEVEL

H
I
M
E
D
L
O

SUPPLY LEVEL

SCRIPTURE

Genesis 2:19-20

SUPPLIES

Bible, unsharpened pencil, plain sheet of paper (optional)

PREPARATION

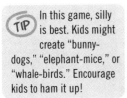

TIP In this game, silly is best. Kids might create "bunny-dogs," "elephant-mice," or "whale-birds." Encourage kids to ham it up!

Rename Game

Kids have fun renaming animals.

Get kids to sit in a circle on the floor. Use an unsharpened pencil as a pointer, and show everyone how to spin it on the floor. The pencil might spin better if placed on a sheet of paper.

Have a child spin the pointer. When the pencil stops spinning, see who the pencil is pointing to. Ask that child to name an animal, such as a kangaroo. Then that child will spin the pointer. When it stops spinning, see who the pencil is pointing to. Have that child name a different animal, such as a cat.

Combine the two animals into a brand-new animal, and have all the kids show how that new animal would move and sound. For example, a "kangaroo-cat" might jump like a kangaroo and meow or purr like a cat.

Play until everyone has contributed to an animal name.

Debrief

At the end of the game, ask:

• *Which of our silly new animals was your favorite, and why?*

Read aloud Genesis 2:19-20.

• *Why do you think God gave Adam the special job of naming animals?*
• *What are some ways we can take care of the animals God created?*

26   **GIANT** BOOK OF GAMES FOR CHILDREN'S MINISTRY

AGES 3-5

What God Made

Kids play a guessing game about
different things God created.

SCRIPTURE

Psalm 33:6-9

SUPPLIES

Bible

PREPARATION

TIP This is a good
outdoor game.

Arrange kids in a circle outside. Say: **I see something God has made. It's white and fluffy, and it's way up high. What do I see?**

When kids answer "a cloud," say: **Yes, God made clouds to give us rain.** Each time they guess a new thing, say what God made that thing for. Play until kids understand the game. Then have them take turns describing and guessing other things that God has made.

Vary the difficulty of the game by offering more or fewer hints.

Debrief

At the end of the game, ask:

- *What was your favorite part of this game?*
- *Why do you think God made so many amazing things for us to enjoy?*

Read aloud Psalm 33:6-9 and say: **Let's thank God for all the things he created.**

Close in prayer, giving thanks to God by letting kids shout out some of the created things that came up during the game.

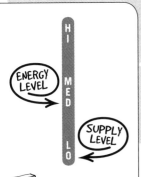

SCRIPTURE

Daniel 6:1-23

SUPPLIES

Bible

PREPARATION

Lion, Lion, Shut Your Mouth

kids explore courage and what happened with Daniel in the lions' den.

Ask for two willing children, one to be the "Angel" of the Lord who shuts the lions' mouths, and the other to be "Daniel." All other kids will be "Lions."

Place the Angel and Daniel at one end of the room, and line up the Lions at the other end. The Lions must crawl on their hands and knees toward Daniel. Encourage them to growl, roar, and paw the air like real lions as they advance toward Daniel. As the closest Lion nears Daniel (and just before the Lion touches Daniel), the Angel will shout loudly, "Lion, Lion, shut your mouth!" All the Lions must crawl as quickly as possible back to the other end of the room and start over.

Have kids take turns playing Daniel and the Angel. Play until everyone has had a turn to be either Daniel or the Angel or as time allows.

Debrief

At the end of the game, discuss the following.

- *Explain what you liked doing best in this game, and why.*
- *Tell about a time you got into trouble for doing something that was right.*
- *What can you do to stand up for what's right this week?*

God's Provision

AGES 3-5

Daniel, the Lions Are Coming

kids get to be Daniel and try to guess which "lion" makes noise.

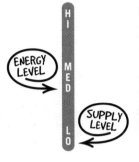

SCRIPTURE
Daniel 6

SUPPLIES
Bible

PREPARATION
none

Open your Bible and summarize the story in Daniel 6 or read it from a children's Bible. Choose one child to be "Daniel." Have Daniel stand on the far side of the room with his back turned to the rest of the kids. Have the other kids pretend to be Lions. They'll quietly creep up and try to touch Daniel before he hears them.

When Daniel hears a noise, he will turn around and point to the Lion he thinks made the noise. If Daniel guesses correctly, that Lion goes back to the starting place. All of the Lions must stop moving until Daniel turns his back to them; then the Lions will move forward again. The first Lion to touch Daniel gets a big hug from him and becomes the next Daniel.

Continue playing until several children have been Daniel.

Debrief

At the end of the game, ask:

- *Explain how you felt being Daniel, knowing that the lions were coming.*
- *What surprised you about getting a hug from a lion?*
- *How does God keep us safe when we're scared?*

AGES 3-5

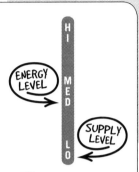

SCRIPTURE

1 Samuel 17

SUPPLIES

Bible

PREPARATION

Ring Around Boy David

Kids celebrate David's victory over Goliath.

O pen your Bible to 1 Samuel 17, and briefly summarize what happened between David and Goliath. Have kids hold hands in a circle with one child in the center as "David."

Say: **Let's celebrate what God did through David. He was a young boy, and God used him to free his entire country from fear.** Lead kids in singing the following verse to the tune of "Ring Around the Rosie":

> *Ring around boy David,*
> *The giant tried to scare him.*
> *David prayed, threw his stone,*
> *and then Goliath fell down!*

Have children fall down at the end. Then have David pick a new David. Continue playing as long as kids are interested.

Debrief

Afterward, ask:

- *What would scare you about facing a giant?*
- *How did God help David?*
- *How can God help us?*

AGES 3-5

Thank You for Sharing

Kids practice their sharing skills with this game of friendly fun.

SCRIPTURE

Acts 2:42-47

SUPPLIES

Bible, small toys or other objects in the room, praise music, music player

PREPARATION

Have children sit in a circle. Read aloud Acts 2:42-47. Say: **The people in the very first church shared what they had with each other. We can share, too! Friends share their toys, their food, and their fun. Let's have fun right now with this sharing game.**

I'm going to give each of you a small toy from our room. When I play praise music, pass the toys around the circle all at once. When I stop the music, look to your neighbors and say, "Thank you for sharing the (name of the toy you're holding)." Help kids get started so they know which direction to pass the toys.

Continue playing as long as kids are having fun. For added excitement, have children pass the toys in opposite directions, with their eyes closed, or as quickly as possible.

Debrief

At the end of the game, discuss the following.

- *What was easy or hard about this game?*
- *Why is it sometimes hard to share things?*
- *What things can you can share with your family and friends this week?*

Say: **Just like the people of the first church shared what they had, we can share what God has given us. Sharing shows our love for God and others.**

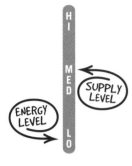

AGES 3-5

Coin Races

Kids relate to the poor widow who gave all she had.

SCRIPTURE

Luke 21:1-4

SUPPLIES

Bible; 10 large, plastic coins and 1 wrapping-paper tube per child; 1 large, plastic bowl

PREPARATION

Place chairs in a tight circle with the backs of the chairs positioned inward.

TIP Don't use small coins for this game — they're a choking hazard. Instead, get large, plastic coins from a discount or craft store to ensure they won't pose a choking risk. Also remind kids that the coins don't belong in their mouths!

Say: **Today we're going to talk about someone who didn't have a lot, but still shared what she had.**

Read aloud Luke 21:1-4.

Say: **Let's play a game where we give our coins like the poor widow.**

Place a large bowl in the center of the chair circle to act as the collection box. Give each child 10 coins and a wrapping-paper tube. (If you don't have wrapping-paper tubes, make tubes by rolling up large pieces of newspaper and taping them.) Show children how to hold their tubes so they rest on the tops of the chair backs and open above the bowl.

Say: **When I say "Go!" put a coin inside the tube, so it rolls down and falls into the bowl. Drop your coins into the bowl one at a time.** Have kids see how many of their coins fall into the bowl.

Debrief

When kids are out of coins, discuss the following.

• *What made it hard to get the coins into the bowl?*
• *What made it hard for the woman to give her coins to God?*
• *How can you give your best to God this week?*

Say: **Even if we don't have any money to give, we can give to God in ways that make him glad.**

What Would You Give?

AGES 3-5

This game helps kids understand why it's important to share.

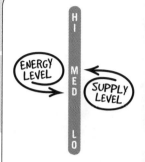

ENERGY LEVEL → SUPPLY LEVEL

HI / MED / LO

Say: **For this game, we'll need coins. Let's make our own.**

Give each child four construction paper coins to decorate with things they treasure.

When everyone's finished, hold your hands out to your side and give thumbs-up with your right hand and thumbs-down with your left. Then say: **I'm going to ask you some questions. If you answer "yes," hop over to my right side where my thumb is up and put down one of your coins. If you answer "no," hop over to my left side where my thumb is down and keep your coins.** After each question, allow time for kids to hop and lay down their coins and then return to their starting places.

Questions to ask:

- *Would you give money to someone who's hungry?*
- *Would you give away food in your refrigerator right before dinner if you thought someone needed it?*
- *Would you send your piggy bank to children who are poor?*
- *Would you give away all your toys to children who don't have any?*

SCRIPTURE

Matthew 10:8

SUPPLIES

Bible, construction paper, markers, scissors

PREPARATION

Cut four circles out of each piece of construction paper (make enough so each child will have four circles).

Debrief

At the end of the game, discuss the following.

- *What do you think it would be like to give away all of your food, or toys, or money?*
- *Tell about something you treasure.*
- *What are some ways we could give things we treasure, like money, food, or toys, to God by sharing them with someone else?*

Say: **God loves it when we give our treasures to him. There are many things we can give, such as toys to a children's hospital, clothes to people who don't have many, or money to our church.**

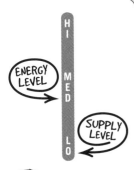

Best for

AGES 3-5

ENERGY LEVEL

H I
M E D
L O

SUPPLY LEVEL

SCRIPTURE

Zechariah 8:16-17

SUPPLIES

Bible, 1 adult or teenage volunteer or helper

PREPARATION

Is It the Truth?

Kids learn the importance of honesty in this fast-paced game.

Say: **The goal of this game is to move forward to touch the "Caller" standing across the room from the starting line.**

Ask your volunteer to be the Caller. The Caller will stand on one side of the room with his or her back turned to kids. Ask the Caller to call out statements such as "Frogs hop," and "Five is a number."

Have kids stand on the opposite side of the room. Say: **If you hear a statement that's true, start tiptoeing toward the Caller. If you hear a statement that's not true (such as "ice is hot"), stop moving and stand still. Let's practice!** Make a few statements that are true or false to let kids get the hang of standing still or tiptoeing forward.

Say: **The Caller might turn around after saying something untrue to see if anyone is moving. Any children caught moving have to go back to the starting line!** Practice a couple rounds to let kids get the hang of it.

As children tag the Caller, they can stand beside the Caller or return to the starting line and play again.

Debrief

At the end of the game, discuss the following.

- *What was this game like for you?*
- *Talk about whether it was easy or hard to believe the Caller.*

Read aloud Zechariah 8:16-17.

- *Why do you think it's important to always tell the truth?*

Say: **God wants us to tell the truth. Let's remember to tell the truth no matter what so people can always believe what we say.**

AGES 3-5

Jesus Came for You

Kids identify mystery speakers and discover that Jesus didn't hide his identity.

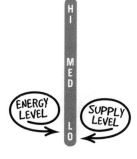

SUPPLIES

chair, blindfold

PREPARATION

Say: **Today we're going to try to sound like different people.**

Blindfold one child and have him or her sit. Let the other children take turns coming up behind the blindfolded child to say, "Jesus came for you!"

Say: **Try to disguise your voice as much as possible. You can say, "Jesus came for you!" in a deep voice, a squeaky voice, like a robot...any way you can think of.**

When the blindfolded child correctly identifies a speaker, a new child gets to take the chair. Play until each child has had a turn in the chair.

Debrief

At the end of the game, discuss the following.

- *Why is it difficult to recognize a voice when it's disguised?*
- *Why do you think some people try to hide who they really are or pretend to be someone else?*
- *Why do you think Jesus didn't try to hide who he was?*

Say: **Jesus didn't hide who he was. He wanted us to know that he came to save us from the punishment of sin.**

Best for

Wisdom

AGES 3-5

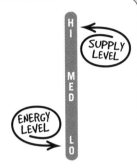
SUPPLY LEVEL

ENERGY LEVEL

SCRIPTURE

Proverbs 2:1-5

SUPPLIES

Bible; sandbox or dishpan full of clean sand; spoons, shovels, and kitchen strainers; small objects kids can take home, such as erasers or small toys (make sure none of the objects poses a choking risk)

PREPARATION

Bury at least three erasers or small toys for every child in the clean sand.

TIP If you don't have access to sand, try hiding treasures in a large cardboard box full of shredded paper.

Sand Search

Kids search for buried treasure to remind them to search for wisdom from God.

Say: **Today we're going to hunt for buried treasure.** Go outside together and give kids tools for their treasure hunt. Explain what they are looking for in the sand.

Make sure each child finds at least one hidden item. If someone doesn't find any items, allow kids to share their treasure and compliment those who behave with generosity.

Say: **Let's count aloud the number of items we found together.** If the kids find all of the treasure and time permits, bury the items and play again. At the end, allow kids to take home their treasures.

Gather the kids and say: **This game is similar to a Bible passage that talks about how we can be wise.** Read aloud Proverbs 2:1-5.

Debrief

At the end of the game, discuss the following.

- *What did you like best about finding treasures?*
- *This Bible passage tells us that learning about God is a treasure. Why is God a treasure to you?*
- *How can we learn more about God?*

Say: **Sometimes you might have questions about what you learn at church or read in the Bible. You can keep learning more by talking to your parents and asking God to help you learn more about him.**

AGES 3-5

Share the Sheep

kids practice sharing with one another.

SCRIPTURE

Genesis 13:8-9

SUPPLIES

Bible, large quantity of pom-poms in two colors, resealable plastic bags, and one piece of colored paper per two kids (paper should match the colors of the pom-poms)

PREPARATION

Say: **God wants us to treat other people the way we want to be treated. One way to practice is to share with others. Let's play a game that reminds us to share and treat others the way we'd like to be treated.**

Help kids pair up and sit on the floor while you read aloud Genesis 13:8-9. Then scatter two different colors of pom-poms on the floor around the room.

Say: **For this game, we're going to pretend that the pom-poms are sheep. You and your partner get to pretend to be Abram and Lot.** Give each pair a plastic bag and a piece of paper that matches a color of pom-pom.

Say: **When I tell you to start, gather as many "sheep" as you can. You'll only keep sheep that match your color of paper. Put those sheep in your bag. If you find sheep of a different color, help other teams by giving them the sheep you find that match their color.**

Lead children in the following rhyme as they play, encouraging them to recite it with you. Say:

> *Sheep! Sheep!*
> *Which ones can*
> *we keep?*

As time allows, let kids switch colors and collect a new color of "sheep" to put in their bags.

Share the Sheep

continued

. . . . Debrief .

At the end of the game, discuss the following.

- *What did you like about collecting sheep with your partner?*
- *What was it like to help other teams?*
- *How did this game help us practice treating others the way we'd like to be treated?*
- *How would you like other people to show you kindness this week?*

Say: **It's important for us to always treat others with kindness. Sharing and helping others is a great way to do that.**

AGES 3-5

Stackin' and Snackin'

Kids stack a snack and name things they're thankful for.

Group kids into trios and hand each trio a paper plate.

Say: **When I say, "Stack 'em high," take turns frosting a cookie and stacking cookies, one on top of the other, on your plate. Each time you stack a cookie, say something you're thankful for. Ready? Stack 'em high!**

Play praise music while kids work. After a few minutes, see how high kids have made their stacks.

Place all of the cookie stacks on the cookie sheet. Then read aloud Psalm 92:1-2 and say: **We can give God thanks because he's good and he loves us forever. God deserves our praise! Look at this stack of thanksgivings! I'm so thankful for all God has given us.**

Let everyone help gobble down the goodies.

Debrief

At the end of the game, discuss the following.

- *What do you like about God?*
- *What can you thank God for during the day? at night?*

SCRIPTURE

Psalm 92:1-2

SUPPLIES

Bible, table, paper plates, cookies, canned frosting, craft sticks or plastic knives to frost cookies, cookie sheet, praise music and player, smocks or old shirts (one per child), antibacterial gel (optional)

PREPARATION

Set the supplies out on a table.

TIP Encourage kids to wash their hands before this game.

ALLERGY ALERT!
See page 8

Best for

AGES 3-5

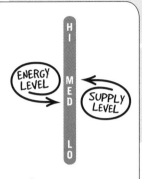

 SCRIPTURE

Mark 4:35-41

 SUPPLIES

Bible, toy boat, bedsheet
(blue if possible)

 PREPARATION

Storm Center

Kids create an indoor "storm" and see how they can trust Jesus.

Say: **Tell about a time you remember being in a big, powerful storm.** (Let several kids share their experiences.) Say: **The same thing happened to Jesus' friends, the disciples! Once, Jesus and the disciples were in a boat on a lake in the middle of a huge storm. Jesus was asleep, but the disciples were so scared, they woke him up. All Jesus had to do was say, "Be still!" and the storm ended.**

Gather the children and stand around a sheet. Have them hold the sheet tightly at waist level with both hands. Place the toy boat on top of the sheet.

Say: **Let's wave the sheet up and down quickly so the boat bounces. This will represent the waves of the storm. When I call out, "Quiet! Be still!" immediately stop waving the sheet.**

Play the game several times.

Debrief

At the end of the game, discuss the following.

- *What things are you afraid of?*
- *Tell about a time you asked Jesus to help you when you were afraid.*
- *What can you do to remember to ask Jesus for help when you're afraid?*

Say: **Jesus protected and cared for the disciples when they were afraid, and he does the same thing for us. Let's remember to ask Jesus for help when we're afraid!**

AGES 3-5

Where's the Special Rock?

Kids remember to praise God for his greatness.

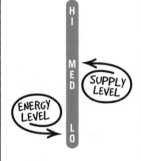

SCRIPTURE

Joshua 4:3-20

SUPPLIES

Bible; three plastic, foam, or paper cups per two children; small rocks

PREPARATION

Read aloud Joshua 4:3-20, then say: **The Israelites crossed the Jordan River on dry ground and set up 12 rocks to remember how God helped them. The rocks helped the Israelites remember to be thankful. People walking by Joshua's rocks knew the rocks were special.**

Today we'll play a guessing game. You'll guess where the special rock is hiding and praise God while you do it! As we play, think of as many great things about God as you can.

Have children find a partner. Give each pair three cups and one rock. Show kids how to hide the rock under one of the three cups. Ask one child from each pair to slide the cups around without lifting them. The children's goal is to confuse their partners. Ask the partners to guess which cup is covering the special rock.

Say: **Each time you find the rock, name something that's great about God, then trade places with your partner and play again.**

· **Debrief** · ·

At the end of the game, discuss the following.

- *Why is it important for us to praise God?*
- *What are ways you can praise God this week?*

AGES 3-5

You're-Special Leis

Kids take home leis that remind them of kind comments from friends.

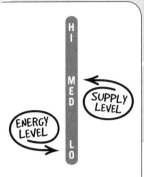

SCRIPTURE

Matthew 10:29-31

SUPPLIES

Bible, ½" x 6" paper strips in bright colors (multiply the number of kids in your group by itself to know how many paper strips you need), glue stick, scissors

PREPARATION

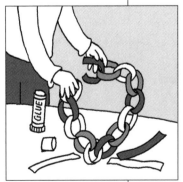

Say: **Today we're going to practice kindness.** Sit in a circle and choose one child to sit in the middle. Have another child take a paper strip and say something nice about the child in the center. If they need it, help kids with ideas such as, "I like to play with you," or "You're my friend."

The child holding the paper strip will make a loop and glue it with the glue stick. Have the next child say something nice to the child in the middle of the circle and thread a paper strip through the looped strip and glue it.

Continue until every child has said something nice to the child in the middle of the circle, and has added a paper strip to the chain. Then give that child a paper strip and a compliment as well. Use your paper strip to join the ends of the chain together to form a lei. If necessary, add more loops to the chain to make it long enough to go over the child's head. Put the lei around the child's neck and say: **Always remember that you're special to our group and to God.**

Choose another child to sit in the middle of the circle. Continue until everyone has a "You're-Special Lei" to wear home.

Say: **I hope you all feel special. You're all very special to God. Let's read in the Bible about how much God loves us.**

Debrief

At the end of the game, read aloud Matthew 10:29-31. Then discuss the following.

• *What was it like when everyone said nice things about* you?
• *What can you do to remember that God thinks you're special?*

Say: **God made you special. You're one-of-a-kind. He loves you very much and gave you friends who care about you.**

Lively Listening

Kids work to improve their listening skills.

AGES 3-5

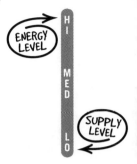

SCRIPTURE

Ephesians 6:1-3

SUPPLIES

Bible, blindfolds (optional)

PREPARATION

Designate one person to be the "Shepherd." Ask three kids to be "False Shepherds." Everyone else will be "Sheep."

Place the Sheep in the center of an open, empty room, and tell them to close their eyes or put on blindfolds. Ask the Shepherd and False Shepherds to silently stand around the perimeter of the room.

Prompt the Shepherd to say, "Come here, Sheep. Come to me." Tell kids to listen closely.

Then allow the False Shepherds to join in, repeating, "Come here, Sheep. Come to me." Tell kids to try to find the one, true Shepherd.

Remind the Sheep to keep their eyes closed as they attempt to find the one true Shepherd. (To make it more challenging for older kids, the Sheep can say "Baa!" as they attempt to find the true Shepherd.)

After playing once, have kids switch roles and play again.

Debrief

Afterward, have kids discuss the following.

- *What were you thinking when you were trying to find the Shepherd?*
- *What was it like to have the distractions of the False Shepherds and the baa-ing from the Sheep?*
- *What distracts you from listening to your parents?*

Say: **It's a challenge to obey your parents when you're surrounded by so many distractions. But God wants us to obey.**

Read aloud Ephesians 6:1-3.

Say: **Let's ask God to help us obey our parents this week.** Close in prayer.

Best for

AGES 3-5

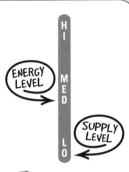

 SCRIPTURE

Luke 15:11-32

 SUPPLIES

Bible

 PREPARATION

The Prodigal Children

Kids have fun acting out the Prodigal Son's return.

Open your Bible to Luke 15:11-32, and summarize the Prodigal Son's experience by saying: **A man had two sons. One son asked his father for some of the family's money. He took the money to live in another town and spent it foolishly. He wasted all the money. Soon, he couldn't even pay for food. He realized he'd made a big mistake and was very sorry. He decided to return home and apologize to his father and ask for a job as a servant. When he returned home, he told his father what he'd done and that he didn't deserve to be called "son" any more. But guess what? Rather than being mad, his father was happy! He threw a huge party to welcome his son home and he forgave him right away. He was happy that his son had returned and learned from his foolish mistakes.**

We're going to play a game to remind us of how happy the father was to see his son.

Form two groups, the Parents and the Children. The Parents will stand on one side of the room and the Children will stand on the other side. On "Go!" have the Children say, "I'm coming home!" Have the Parents respond, "We're so happy because we've missed you!"

Then have the Children and the Parents all hop to the middle of the room. Each Parent will pair up with a Child by linking arms, then skip or walk around in circles. Then signal the pairs to stop, and have Parents and Children return to opposite sides of the room.

Have kids switch roles and play again.

Debrief

At the end of the game, ask:

- *Why do you think the dad was happy to see his son?*
- *What's it like for you when you are away from your mom or dad?*
- *Why is it important to love our family members, no matter what?*

The Beautiful Feet That Bring Good News

Kids take off their shoes and socks for this game about delivering good news.

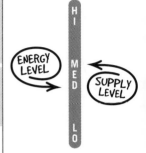

AGES

Ask kids to remove their socks and shoes. Keeping them together, place them along a wall. Form two groups and that will line up on opposite sides of the room.

Say: **The Bible says that the feet that bring good news are beautiful because they carry such an important message. Let's deliver the good news with our feet.**

Give the card with the words "Good news!" to the first person in one of the lines.

Say: **Put the card between your toes and walk across the room. Then give the card to the first person in the other line and go to the back of that line. The next player will walk across the room with the card between his or her toes, give the card to the next person in the other line, and join the back of that line.**

If the card falls from between a child's toes, have him or her replace it, but don't insist that the child start over. Stay close to the child walking to help as needed.

Continue until everyone has had at least one turn to deliver the good news.

SCRIPTURE

Isaiah 52:7

SUPPLIES

index cards, markers

PREPARATION

Draw a heart or write the words "Good news!" on an index card, and fold the card in half.

Debrief

At the end of the game, discuss the following.

- *What was easy or difficult about delivering the card in this game?*
- *Why is it important for others to learn about Jesus?*
- *How can you tell others that Jesus loves them?*

Say: **Not only can we use our feet, but we can also use our hearts and heads to figure out new ways to let others know that Jesus loves them!**

Best for

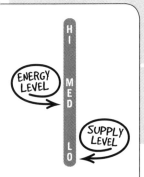
AGES 3-5

ENERGY LEVEL

HI MED LO

SUPPLY LEVEL

SCRIPTURE

Mark 10:24-25

SUPPLIES

Bible, needle (optional)

PREPARATION

The Eye of the Needle

Kids learn about the importance of faith as they go through the "eye of a needle."

Say: **Jesus said that it's easier for a camel to go through the eye of a needle than it is for a rich man to enter the kingdom of God. Let's pretend that we're camels with humps and we're trying to get through the tiny eye of a needle.**

Read aloud Mark 10:24-25 and explain to kids what the eye of a needle is if they don't know—even better, show them a needle so they can see how small the eye is. Arrange the children in one single-file line in the middle of the room with their legs spread to form a tunnel.

Have the last child in line drop to his or her knees and crawl through the tunnel, or "eye of the needle."

Say: **When you get through the tunnel, stand up, join the line, and say, "This camel made it." That's the signal for the next child at the back of the line to drop to his or her knees and crawl through the eye of the needle.**

Play for several minutes. See how fast the children can thread their way through the needle.

Debrief

At the end of the game, discuss the following.

- *What was easy or difficult about this game?*
- *When is it hard to give away your favorite things, like toys or treats?*
- *Why does God want us to put him first, before our toys and other favorite things? How could you do that this week?*

Say: **Heaven is better than anything we have here on earth. And God wants us to put him first, before anything else, so we can be with him in heaven. The rich young man didn't understand that we must be willing to completely follow Jesus. Let's remember to put God first.**

AGES 3-5

How Do I Feel?

Kids learn to identify their feelings and realize that Jesus takes away fears.

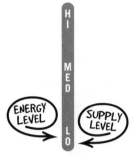

SUPPLIES

PREPARATION

With kids sitting in pairs on the floor across from each other, read aloud the following prompts. Pause after you read each of the following statements to allow time for their responses.

- *Show what your face would look like if you were angry.*
- *Show what your face would look like if you were happy.*
- *Show what your face would look like if you were sad.*
- *Show what your face would look like if you were scared.*

Say: **Now I'm going to say some things that could happen. Decide how you'd feel if these things happened to you, then look at your partner and make a face to show how you'd feel. Do this as fast as you can!**

Read each of the following situations aloud. Pause after each statement so kids can make faces that show how they'd feel.

- *You drop your ice cream cone.*
- *It's Christmas morning, and it's time to open presents.*
- *You fall down and cut your knee.*
- *You hear a strange noise during the night.*

After you've given these scenarios, say: **Now we'll switch things around. I'm going to say the same things, but I want you to make a face that's the opposite of how you'd feel.** Explain "opposite" if necessary.

Go back through the scenarios. Expect lots of giggles as kids mix up their expressions.

Debrief

Afterward, ask:

- *What was this game like for you?*
- *What can you do when you feel sad or scared?*
- *How can it make us feel better to tell Jesus about our fears?*

AGES 3-5

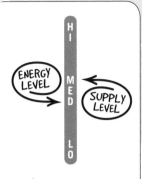

Follow Me

This fun, easy game will help young children
learn about ways to follow God.

SCRIPTURE

John 8:12

SUPPLIES

Bible, flashlight, pieces
of rope or yarn

PREPARATION

Read aloud John 8:12. Say: **The Bible says God is light. And God wants us to follow him.**

Form pairs. Help partners tie together one leg each so each duo becomes three-legged. Turn off the light to make the room dark. Have each pair try to catch the light of a flashlight as you shine it in different directions. Maneuver the light so kids have to change directions frequently.

Play as long as time permits and children remain interested. When you are finished playing, turn the lights back on.

Debrief

Gather everyone and sit on the floor to discuss the following.

- *What did you like about following the light?*
- *What was difficult about following the light?*
- *What did you do to help each other follow the light?*
- *What can you do to help each other follow God?*

Say: **We can help each other follow God by praying for each other and by coming to church.**

AGES 3-5

Runaway Game

Kids learn about how Jonah experienced God's forgiveness.

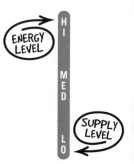

SCRIPTURE

Jonah 1–3

SUPPLIES

Bible, small object such as a plastic ball or toy

PREPARATION

Organize kids into a circle, and ask them to put their hands behind their backs. Choose someone to be "Jonah," and give Jonah an object such as a plastic ball or small toy. Jonah will carry the object around the outside of the circle while everyone else says:

> *Jonah, Jonah disobeyed.*
> *God forgave him anyway.*

At the end of the phrase, Jonah will put the object into another person's hands. That person will chase Jonah around the circle. If Jonah makes it back to the open spot in the circle without being tagged, the person holding the object will be Jonah, and the game begins all over again.

Debrief

After the game, open your Bible to the book of Jonah. Show kids the words.

Say: **In the Bible we read how God told Jonah to deliver an important message for God, but instead, Jonah ran away. Jonah got on a boat as he was trying to hide from God—but God always knew where Jonah was. God brought a big storm, and Jonah ended up in the water where a big fish swallowed him. God kept Jonah safe inside the fish. Jonah asked God to forgive him, and God did. The big fish spat out Jonah on the beach, and then Jonah followed God's instructions.**

Discuss the following together.

- *Why do you sometimes disobey?*
- *Why do you think Jonah couldn't hide from God when he was trying to disobey what God told him to do?*
- *What do you think about God forgiving Jonah?*

Say: **God forgave Jonah, and he'll forgive us, too. He's our loving God.**

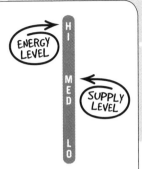

ENERGY LEVEL

SUPPLY LEVEL

HI
MED
LO

SCRIPTURE

Luke 10:27-28

SUPPLIES

Bible, 15 adhesive bandages and one cup of water per group of four kids

PREPARATION

A Friend in Need

Kids help someone who's unable to pay them back.

Use this game to illustrate how Jesus wants us to take care of each other. Form teams of four. Choose one person from each team to be the "Friend" in need. Have the Friends go to the opposite end of the room from their teams and lie down. They may even want to pretend to need help as they wait. Give the remaining children on each team a supply of 15 adhesive bandages and a cup of water.

On "Go!" teams race with their supplies to their "hurt" team members. The goal is to put 15 bandages on the Friend, give him or her a drink of water, and carry the Friend back to the starting point. (Younger kids can each hug their Friend instead.)

Debrief

Once every team has accomplished this, read aloud Luke 10:27-28. Ask:

- *What was this game like for you?*
- *Tell about a time someone helped you.*
- *What can you do to help others?*

Best for

AGES 3-5

Let It Shine

Kids celebrate their talents and understand that their gifts come from God.

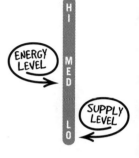
ENERGY LEVEL

SUPPLY LEVEL

Say: **Think of something you can do well. Maybe you can make a special silly face or are really good at something.**

Allow children some time to think of a special talent they have or something they'd like to be. Then say: **God gives everyone special gifts, and God wants us to share our gifts with others. Let's take turns sharing our gifts.**

Arrange kids in a circle and turn off most of the lights. Sing "This Little Light of Mine" together. During the song, have kids take turns making the flashlight beam wiggle on the walls and ceilings.

> *This little light of mine,*
> *I'm gonna let it shine.*
> *This little light of mine,*
> *I'm gonna let it shine.*
> *This little light of mine,*
> *I'm gonna let it shine,*
> *Let it shine, let it shine, let it shine.*
>
> *Hide it under a bushel, NO!*
> *I'm gonna let it shine.*
> *Won't let Satan blow it out,*
> *I'm gonna let it shine.*
> *Let it shine 'till Jesus comes,*
> *I'm gonna let it shine,*
> *Let it shine, let it shine, let it shine.*

After the song, take the flashlight and shine it on each child (not in his or her eyes) as he or she acts out a talent. You can even make up an exciting commentary to go with each performance, and include affirmations. For example, if Rosie acts out ice skating, you might say,

SCRIPTURE

Romans 12:6-8

SUPPLIES

Bible, flashlight

PREPARATION

"**And now in the spotlight is Rosie, the world's greatest ice skater. Watch as she skates a figure eight. See how she can balance on one leg without falling. Let's give a big hand to Rosie!**" Encourage the children to clap after each performance.

Play until each child has had a turn in the spotlight and has been affirmed.

Debrief

At the end of the game, discuss the following.

- *What was it like to be in the spotlight?*
- *What were you surprised to learn about other kids?*

Read aloud Romans 12:6-8, and focus on the beginning: "God has given us different gifts." Then ask:

- *What would it be like if we all had the same talent?*
- *How can we use our talents to praise and serve God?*

Camel Run

In this relay, kids deliver treasures and learn about the wise men.

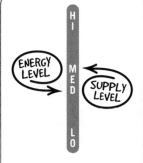

AGES 3-5

Form trios and say: **After Jesus was born, some wise men traveled a long way to bring him wonderful gifts. In this game, we can pretend to be wise men bringing gifts on our camels! But first, you'll need to choose someone in your group to be the "Camel." The other two will be "Wise Men."**

When groups have their Camels, give each trio three treasure bags, and have everyone line up along one wall. Instruct the Camels to get on their hands and knees. Have the two Wise Men stand on either side of their Camel.

Tell each pair of Wise Men to put one of their treasure bags on their Camel's back and put the other two bags on the floor. Have all of the Camels crawl as the Wise Men walk to carefully deliver their treasure bags to the opposite side of the room. The Wise Men will help keep the bags from falling off of the Camels' backs. The Wise Men will set the bags on the floor, then the trios will travel back to get another treasure bag.

Let a different child be the Camel on each of the next trips. Continue the game until all the treasure bags are delivered.

 Debrief

After the game, ask the trios to sit together, open their bags, and enjoy their tasty treasures while you discuss the following.

- *What was this game like for you?*
- *Why do you think people brought gifts to Jesus when he was born?*
- *What gifts can we give Jesus today?*

 **SCRIPTURE**

Matthew 2:1-12

 SUPPLIES

Bible, one paper lunch sack per child, jellybeans, tape or stapler

 **PREPARATION**

Fill paper lunch sacks with small handfuls of jellybeans (or some other treat). Fold the top of the bags down, then tape or staple them shut.

ALLERGY ALERT!
See page 8

Best for

AGES 3-5

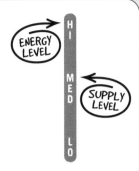

ENERGY LEVEL

HI MED LO

SUPPLY LEVEL

You Can't Keep Jesus Down

Kids discover that even though people tried to keep Jesus in the grave, they couldn't!

SUPPLIES

one large, rectangular laundry basket (the horizontal kind); six non-latex, helium balloons with long strings that all fit inside the laundry basket; one thick towel or blanket heavy enough to keep the balloons inside the laundry basket

PREPARATION

Before kids arrive, place the helium balloons inside the laundry basket, and cover them with the towel or blanket.

TIP These supplies are for a group of up to six children. If you have a larger group, form groups of up to six, and give each group the above supplies.

BALLOON WARNING! See page 8

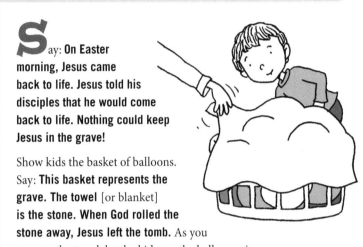

Say: **On Easter morning, Jesus came back to life. Jesus told his disciples that he would come back to life. Nothing could keep Jesus in the grave!**

Show kids the basket of balloons.

Say: **This basket represents the grave. The towel** [or blanket] **is the stone. When God rolled the stone away, Jesus left the tomb.** As you remove the towel, let the kids see the balloons rise.

Say: **The object of this game is to try to get the balloons back into the basket. Each of you may use only one hand. You must keep your other hand behind your back. Work together to capture all the balloons. Ready? Go!**

Debrief

After playing, gather everyone and discuss the following.

• *Explain whether this game was easy or hard for you.*
• *What kind of power does Jesus have to be able to come back to life?*
• *Why do you think we celebrate Easter?*

Say: **Jesus has more power than anything or anyone. He's so powerful, he came back to life so we could live with him in heaven. Easter is a time to celebrate Jesus' power!**

AGES 3-5

Belly Laugh

This silly game reminds kids that
God loves a joyful heart.

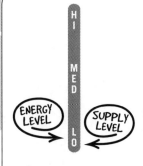

SUPPLIES

PREPARATION

Beginning at the edge of your room, ask one child to lie on his or her back. Then have another child lie with his or her head on the first child's belly and feet pointing into the middle of the room. The remaining kids can lie down one at a time with their heads resting on the previous child's belly. Once kids are in position, you'll have a formation similar to a caterpillar on the floor.

Choose one person to start the game by shouting "Ha!" The next person will shout "Ha, ha!" and each child will continue to add a "ha" as they work around the group. Sooner or later, the group will burst into laughter, causing heads to bounce on bellies with joy.

· *Debrief* · ·

Afterward, discuss the following.

- *What was fun about playing this game?*
- *What makes you laugh?*
- *Why do you think God gives us the gifts of joy and laughter?*

Close by letting kids take turns telling a funny story or joke. Say: **God wants us to experience joy and fun every day!**

Best for

AGES 3-5

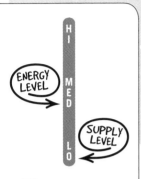

ENERGY LEVEL

SUPPLY LEVEL

SCRIPTURE

Exodus 14:15-31

SUPPLIES

Bible

PREPARATION

Part the Sea

Kids play follow the Leader as they learn about Moses.

Open your Bible to Exodus, and summarize how God parted the Red Sea. Say: **When Moses led his people out of Egypt toward a new land and new life, angry Egyptian soldiers chased after them. Moses and his people, who'd been slaves to the Egyptians, were cornered at the edge of the Red Sea. They couldn't get around the water. God told Moses to raise his hand over the sea and he would make a path for the people to pass through so Moses could lead them. Moses followed God's instructions, and the water of the Red Sea parted and opened a path for the people to walk through to the other side. When the angry Egyptians came charging behind them, God closed the water back over them and saved Moses and his people.**

Choose one child to be "Moses." With the rest of the kids lined up behind Moses, have Moses say:

God was good; he parted the sea.
Come on, Israelites, follow me!

Help Moses choose an action to use while leading the other children around the room, such as walking on tiptoes or hopping. Encourage the others to imitate Moses as they follow him once around the room. After a little while, choose another child to be Moses and repeat the game.

Play until everyone has had a chance to be Moses.

Debrief

Afterward, discuss the following.

• *What did you like about being Moses?*
• *What can we do to follow God like Moses did?*

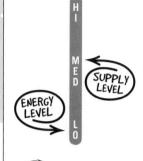

AGES 3-5

Puzzled

Kids identify with Noah the ark-builder as they work with their friends to complete a challenging task.

Distribute the boxed puzzles to a few kids, and have them dump the pieces into the tub. Invite the others to thoroughly mix the contents of the tub.

Say: **Noah obeyed God when he built a huge boat and gathered the animals as God instructed him. Our challenge is to build all these animal puzzles. We'll work in groups to sort the pieces and complete all the puzzles.**

Form one group per puzzle, and assign each group a puzzle. Give each group their puzzle box so they have a picture to work from. Observe kids' progress and intermittently offer hints such as: "Cooperate with the other groups first to sort all the pieces before you begin," or "Work on the corners and edges first."

Set a time limit based on how much time you have available; for example, you might let kids work for between five and 15 minutes.

When the puzzles are finished or time is up, congratulate kids for their fine work. Then have them sit while you read aloud Genesis 6:12-16. Then discuss these questions.

- *What was easiest about this challenge? What was most difficult?*
- *Explain whether you think building the ark would be an easy or hard task.*

Say: **God trusts us and gives us big assignments sometimes. Thankfully, he doesn't expect us to complete them all alone! God gives us faithful people who help.**

SCRIPTURE

Genesis 6:12-16

SUPPLIES

Bible; several boxed animal puzzles of similar size and difficulty (five to 50 pieces, depending on the ages of your kids); tub or box large enough to hold all the puzzle pieces

PREPARATION

AGES 3-5

SCRIPTURE

Genesis 9:12-16

SUPPLIES

Bible, sock, bag of cotton batting, long strips of rainbow-colored ribbon

PREPARATION

Fill the toe of a sock with cotton batting to the size of an orange. Tie a knot in the sock just above the batting. Tie ribbons to the sock so they trail behind it when the sock is tossed.

Rainbow Ball

Kids remember that God promises to take care of them.

Read aloud Genesis 9:12-16. Have kids form two groups and stand on either side of the room.

Say: **God promises to always be with us. He was with Noah and he is with us, too. That doesn't mean life will always be easy, but it will never be too much for us to handle with God's help.**

Show kids how the ball creates a rainbow when thrown across the room. Let each child try throwing the ball to the other group.

Say: **The object of the game is to pass the ball so it makes a rainbow in the air to help us remember God's promises.**

Each time someone throws the ball, ask that person to say how God has kept his promise to be with them always. It could be a fun memory with their family, playing with a friend yesterday, or a favorite toy. After mentioning their blessing, that child will throw the ball to someone else on the other side of the room.

Debrief

Afterward, ask:

- *What's your favorite thing about rainbows—and why?*
- *God reminded Noah of his promise through a rainbow. What can you do to remember that God always keeps his promises?*

Say: **The rainbow is a sign that God always keeps his promises. God promises to always care for us!**

AGES 3-5

All That I Am

Kids learn to make it their first priority to know and love God.

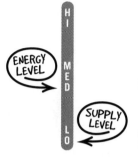

Gather kids in a circle and say: **I have a surprise for you today—a truly delicious surprise. All the surprises are hidden somewhere in this room, and there's a surprise for everyone. I'm going to let you search for them. When you find one, bring it back to this circle and hold on to it. Only find and bring back one surprise. Ready? Go!**

SCRIPTURE

Psalm 150, Psalm 103:2

SUPPLIES

Bible, bag of individually wrapped treats

Debrief

As children enjoy their treats, ask:

* *When I said "Go!" why did you hurry?*
* *What's your very favorite thing to do—something you like doing more than anything else?*

Read aloud Psalm 150. Then ask:

* *Why is it important that we take time to praise God?*
* *What do you do when you praise God?*

Read aloud Psalm 103:2. Say: **Turn to a friend and tell one way you'll praise God this week.**

PREPARATION

Choose a treat that's a favorite of your kids. Before kids arrive, hide the treats around the room. You'll need one treat for each child.

ALLERGY ALERT!
See page 8

AGES 3-5

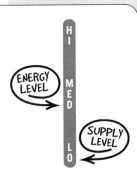

Path of Praises

children practice saying kind things to each other.

SCRIPTURE

John 12:12-13

SUPPLIES

Bible, party horns or rhythmic instruments (optional)

PREPARATION

TIP This game will be even more fun if you let the children blow party horns or play rhythmic instruments to add to their cheers.

Place children in two lines so that each child faces a partner in the opposite line. Be sure there is enough space between them so the lines extend from one end of your room to the other.

Say: **Once when Jesus rode into Jerusalem, everyone praised him and shouted good things about him. We've made a road here between our two lines. Let's do the same and say good things about our friends as they walk down this path of praises.**

Ask the children to raise their arms and wiggle their hands and fingers as the first child from one of the lines walks down the path. As he or she is walking, have the other children yell cheers such as "Hooray!" and "Yay, [child's name]!"

When the child reaches the end of the road, have him or her rejoin the line. Then have the first child from the other line walk down the path. Continue until everyone has walked down the path of praises.

Debrief

At the end of the game, ask:

- *What was it like to hear praises from people?*
- *What did you like about giving praises?*
- *In what ways can we praise Jesus every day?*

AGES 3-5

Hide and Find

Kids play a following game, and think about
how to follow God's directions.

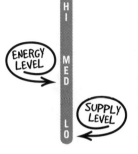

Tell kids to form a circle.

Say: **Great job following directions! Let's play a game to help us remember that God helps us obey him. Find two partners.**

Help kids form trios, and provide each trio with a small toy.

Say: **I'll walk by your group and tap one of you on the head. If you feel me tap your head, you will close your eyes. While your eyes are closed, one partner will hide the toy in the room while the other partner watches where the toy is hidden.**

Tap one child from each group, and help a different child hide his or her team's item.

When everyone is finished, say: **Keep your eyes closed. Now your other partner will walk beside you and guide you by giving directions until you find the toy.**

Encourage partners to give clues and simple directions to help the other children find the hidden toys. Tell kids to keep their eyes closed as their partners guide them. Remind children to give directions such as, "Walk over to the dollhouse," or "Turn left," as they guide their partners.

Once kids find the toys, have them swap roles and play again.

Debrief

After the game, discuss:

- *What was this game like for you?*
- *How did your partners help you?*
- *How was having a partner help you like having God help you?*
- *Why do you think it's important to follow God's directions?*

 SCRIPTURE

Psalm 119:105-106

 SUPPLIES

Bible, one small toy for every three children

 **PREPARATION**

Hide and Find
continued

Say: **God loves us and gives us good directions. When we follow God's directions and obey him, we'll be happy. Sometimes it may seem hard to obey God's directions. But just like our partners walked with us while they guided us, God helps us obey him so we know what to do. Anytime a rule seems hard for you to follow, you can ask God to help you.**

Early Elementary GAMES

Mention that you're about to play a game with kids this age, and you'll see their eyes light up with a spark of interest. Kids between the ages of 6 and 9 are busy working on their relationships with one another, and games are a perfect way to support this developmental need for friendship and fun.

Each game in this section is built for early elementary kids and focuses on noncompetitive participation to elicit laughter and friendship—all while strengthening kids' faith and reinforcing a specific Bible point.

Ready to have some fun?

Best for

AGES 6-9

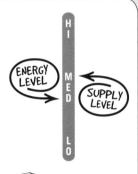

ENERGY LEVEL

SUPPLY LEVEL

HI MED LO

SCRIPTURE

Jeremiah 29:11-13

SUPPLIES

Bible, a different 10- to 15-piece puzzle (created for young children) for every three or four kids, small gifts (such as stickers or candy)

PREPARATION

Place each puzzle's pieces in its box, but take one piece from each puzzle and place it in one of the other puzzle boxes.

ALLERGY ALERT!
See page 8

Everyone Fits

Kids learn that everyone has a place in God's plans.

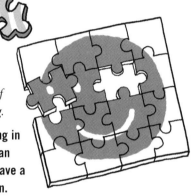

Ask kids to discuss the following, and be prepared to share some of your own experiences.

- *Describe a time you felt out of place or like you didn't belong.*

Say: **No matter what's happening in our lives, God has a special plan for every one of us. We each have a place to fit in God's master plan.**

Read aloud Jeremiah 29:11-13. Form groups of three or four. Give each group a puzzle and say: **The first group to complete its puzzle gets a prize.**

When the kids comment about the misfit piece in their box, say: **Even though that piece may not seem valuable to you, it's very important to the completion of another group's puzzle.**

Have kids figure out which group needs the misfit pieces. When they've finished the puzzles, have the kids sit in a circle.

Debrief

After the game, ask:

- *What was easy or difficult about this experience?*
- *Describe what it means to you to know that you have a purpose in God's plan, just like the special puzzle piece.*

Give every child a treat and say: **We're all unique and special in God's eyes! He loves us and has good plans for each of us.**

AGES 6-9

Bible Smuggle

Kids pass around a Bible to explore
the value of God's Word.

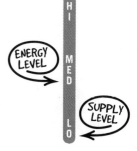

SCRIPTURE

2 Timothy 3:16-17

SUPPLIES

small Bible

PREPARATION

Start in a circle with kids holding their hands behind their backs. Choose someone to be "It." Move It to the center of the circle. Hand a small Bible to one person standing in the circle. Have that person secretly pass the Bible to someone else behind his or her back. Encourage kids to try to confuse the person in the middle so he or she doesn't know where the Bible is. Kids could pretend to pass the Bible back and forth.

After a few minutes, have It guess who's holding the Bible. If caught, that person becomes It. If not, have It guess again. Play several rounds.

Debrief

After the game, sit down together.

Say: **In some countries, it's against the law to have a Bible. So Christians smuggle—or sneak—Bibles into these countries. Many people risk their lives so people can have a Bible.**

Discuss the following.

- *What was it like to try to hide the Bible?*
- *Why is the Bible important to us as Christians?*
- *What can you do this week to make the Bible part of your life?*

Close by reading aloud 2 Timothy 3:16-17 and thanking God for the gift of his Word.

Best for

AGES 6-9

Who's Who?

This icebreaker will get kids talking and learning about different people from the Bible.

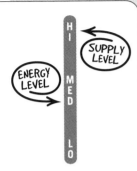

SUPPLIES

one 3x5 index card; one strip of paper per child; pencil; tape; scissors

PREPARATION

Cut strips of paper and tape them together to make a paper headband for each child. On each 3x5 card, write the name of one person from the Bible (for example, Jesus, Mary, Joseph, God, Noah, Moses, David, Rachel, Jonah, Judas, and Lazarus)

Help kids each put on a paper headband. Tape a card with a name to each person's headband without kids seeing the names. Then provide everyone a master list of names so kids have some idea of who they might be. Give kids five minutes to go around the group, asking only yes-or-no questions to try to discover their identity.

Give kids these hints: Their questions could begin broad, such as "Am I a boy? Am I a girl?" Then questions can get more specific, such as "Am I in Jesus' family?" "Did I build something?" For added fun, include factoids about each person on the list to give kids fodder for formulating their questions.

Debrief

After kids have guessed their identities, discuss the following.

- *How easy or difficult was it to discover your person, and why?*
- *Why is it important to "get to know" the people throughout the Bible?*

AGES 6-9

Bushel of Books

As kids collect books, they'll remember
that the Bible is an important book.

SCRIPTURE

Luke 24:44-45

SUPPLIES

Bible, three baskets or
boxes, large quantity of
books (approximately
three per child)

PREPARATION

Form three groups and have each group stand in a line at the same end of the room as everyone else.

Say: **The object of this game is to collect all the books into baskets.**

Behind each group, stack at least three books per child. Place the baskets about 10 feet away from the front of the lines.

Say: **Each person will take a turn putting a book on your head and walking to the basket. After your turn, take the book off of your head and carefully place it in the basket. Be careful not to drop the book at any time, but if you do, put it back on your head and keep going. Then you'll run back to your group, and the next person will take a turn.**

Add variety by assigning kids different ways to carry books on their heads to the starting line, such as crab walking, hopping, or walking backward. When one group finishes, have those kids help another group carry all their books to a basket. If time allows, continue to have all books carried on top of kids' heads; even the kids who are helping.

Debrief

After the game, discuss the following.

- *What was it like to get all the books into the basket?*
- *Why are we careful with books?*

Hold up a Bible. Ask:

- *Why is God's book so important?*
- *Explain whether you'd play the game we just did using Bibles rather than regular books.*
- *Why should we be careful with the Bible?*

Say: **God wants us to know about him and live a life that honors him. He tells us how in the Bible. It's one very important book!**

AGES 6-9

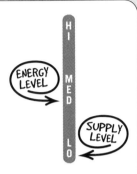

Sitting Circles

Kids work together to discover the importance of the entire body of Christ.

SCRIPTURE

1 Corinthians 12:26-27

SUPPLIES

Bible

PREPARATION

Arrange kids in a circle facing inward and standing shoulder to shoulder. Then have everyone turn to the right so they're standing behind the person next to them.

Say: **Our first task is to form a sitting circle. Once we do that, I'm going to give you a job to do. You must do your job while staying connected with everyone else in the group.**

Instruct everyone to slowly sit down on the knees of the person behind him or her until everyone is sitting in a circle. This may require several tries! If your group is large, you may form more than one circle or challenge kids to form one huge circle.

Once the circle is formed, say: **Good job, everyone! Now let's exercise a few body parts without breaking the circle. Nod your head at me.** Pause. **That was too easy! Wave your right hand at me.** Pause. **I think you're ready for something a lot more challenging. Kick your right leg out to the side and back again.**

Respond according to what happens to the circle. Make up a few more silly instructions.

Say: **Now for a real job! Are you ready?**

Give the group a task to accomplish, such as moving together to turn off a light or picking up a piece of paper on the floor and throwing it away. Kids must move as a group. If someone falls out of the circle, the entire group must stop and wait until everyone is seated again. The job isn't considered finished unless it's done with everyone seated in the circle.

Debrief

After playing this game, ask kids to form trios and discuss the following.

- *Describe whether it was easy or difficult to do things as a group.*
- *What happened when one part of the Sitting Circle fell or couldn't keep up? What happened when everyone worked and moved together?*

Read aloud 1 Corinthians 12:26-27.

- *How is this experience like or unlike what the Scripture says about our role in the body of Christ?*
- *How important was each person in this experience? Explain.*

Close in prayer, thanking God that we are all important parts of the body of Christ.

AGES 6-9

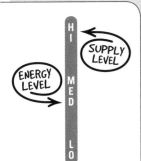

Bucket Brigade

kids Discover that God wants to share Jesus with everyone.

SCRIPTURE

John 4:5-42

SUPPLIES

Bible, two large buckets, water, one paper cup for each child, timer or stopwatch, plastic sheet to protect the floor (optional)

PREPARATION

Fill one of the buckets halfway with water. Place the two buckets on the ground about 10 feet apart (adjust the distance if you have lots of kids). If you're playing indoors, consider spreading a plastic sheet on the floor where you'll play. Before you begin playing, test to ensure the surface isn't slippery when wet.

Say: **One woman who met Jesus wanted to tell all her friends what he said about "living water"—or eternal life. Jesus told her that being friends with him was like enjoying a cool, refreshing glass of water and that by believing in him, she would have eternal life. The woman wanted to share her joy with everyone she knew. Let's play a game to get us thinking about the people we can share living water with.**

Have kids stand in a line between the two buckets. Give each child a paper cup.

Say: **Let's pretend this bucket of water is Jesus' living water. The empty bucket will be our friends who don't know Jesus yet. Let's try to move as much of the water as we can in three minutes. When I say "Go!" the person standing closest to the water will scoop water out of the bucket and share it with the next person in line. Keep passing the water from one person's cup to the next until the last person pours it into the empty bucket. Let's see how much water we can move.**

Set the timer for three minutes, and shout "Go!" When time is up, gather kids around the second bucket and celebrate how much water they moved.

· (Debrief) · ·

At the end of the game, discuss the following.

· *Why do you think the woman wanted to share what Jesus told her about eternal life with all her friends?*
· *Why is it important for you to tell all your friends about Jesus?*
· *Who can you tell about Jesus this week?*

Say: **It's a wonderful thing to be friends with Jesus! We can be like the woman in the Bible and tell everyone we know about eternal life with Jesus.**

Best for

AGES 6-9

Concentration Conversation

Kids play a zany acting game and learn that Jesus taught us how to pray.

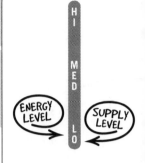

SCRIPTURE

Matthew 6:5-13

SUPPLIES

Bible, two chairs

PREPARATION

Set two chairs close together, facing each other.

Say: **In this wacky acting game, you'll form two groups, and each group will choose one actor. The actors will act out a scene I give you. But here's the twist: The rest of you will tell the actors what to say next. The actors will repeat what you call out. Remember, you can provide funny lines, but all suggestions must be kind and God-honoring. You'll all take turns being actors and audience members.**

Choose a scene from the scene starters below, or make up one of your own. Assign each actor his or her role. Have the children in groups take turns telling their actors what to say. Continue for a minute or so, then change actors and either continue the scene or switch to a new one. Repeat until everyone has had a turn to act.

> Scene Starters:
> • A child approaches a grouchy cashier to buy a candy bar.
> • Two children decide who gets the first turn at a video game.
> • A parent tells a child to go and clean his or her bedroom.
> • A teacher catches a student cheating on a test.
> • Two children are riding bikes and one child gets a flat tire.

Debrief

At the end of the game, discuss the following.

- *Describe what it was like to be told what to say.*
- *Describe a time you were in a situation where you didn't know what you should say next.*
- *How do you know what to say to God when you pray?*

Say: **Jesus' friends weren't sure what they should say to God when they were praying, so they asked for Jesus' help. Jesus was happy to teach them how to talk with God and be friends with him. Jesus teaches us how to talk with God, too. Here's what he said.**

Read aloud Matthew 6:5-13, then close by having kids pray with you.

Best for

AGES 6-9

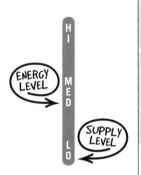

ENERGY LEVEL

SUPPLY LEVEL

SUPPLIES

PREPARATION

Do Your Part

kids see that they have a responsibility
to share their faith with others.

Have kids form groups of four. If you can't make groups of four, give multiple kids one role, or give each person multiple roles. In each group, assign the following body parts: one child will be the torso, one the head, one the arms and hands, and one the legs and feet.

Say: **Each group is going to be a "Body." I'm going to give each Body a task to do. Your group must work together to perform the task, but each person may only perform the movement for his or her specific "body part."**

If you have a large number of kids, give all groups the same task to try simultaneously. If you have a smaller group, let groups take turns performing different tasks.

Say: **Your group needs to stand close together so you can perform your Body tasks together well. Remember that the head, or brain, always goes first, because it controls the rest of the body.**

Suggest that groups perform the tasks of marching in place, doing jumping jacks, or moving a book from one spot to another. Leave it to groups to work out how they'll perform each task; there's not a right or wrong way.

After all groups are done, lead kids in a round of applause for everyone's participation.

Debrief

At the end of the game, discuss the following.

- *Tell why doing your group's task was easier or more difficult than you expected.*

Do Your Part
continued

- *What would happen if someone wasn't able to do his or her part in the Body?*
- *How is this experience like or unlike what happens when we're good examples of our faith in Jesus to others?*
- *Why is it sometimes harder than we expect to be good examples of our faith?*

Say: **Jesus wants us to share our faith with others. He wants everyone with him in heaven. And he wants his followers to work together and be good examples of our faith for others to see.**

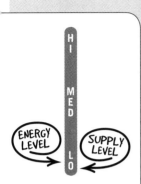

Best for

AGES 6-9

ENERGY LEVEL

SUPPLY LEVEL

HI MED LO

SCRIPTURE

Luke 5:19-20;
John 8:3-11

SUPPLIES

Bible

PREPARATION

Five in a Row

*Kids discover their sins are forgotten
when Jesus forgives them.*

Bring five children to the front of the group. Ask them to leave the room, change something minor about their appearance, and return. Kids might do things like switch shoes or remove a hair clip or trade glasses before they re-enter the room. Challenge the rest of the group to discern what's different about the kids. When the group figures out the correct changes, choose five other children to repeat the game.

Debrief

At the end of the game, discuss the following.

- *How did you remember what was different about your friends in the game?*
- *What kinds of things do you wish other people would remember about you?*
- *Why are some things easier to remember about people than others?*
- *What things do you wish they wouldn't remember?*

Say: **Sometimes we wish people wouldn't remember certain things about us—we want them to remember only good things! That's like when we ask Jesus to forgive us for the wrong things we do—and he remembers the good things about us, not the bad!**

AGES 6-9

Trash Toss

Kids learn why trusting God is important through Jonah's experience.

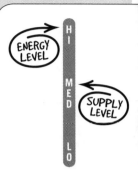

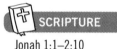

SCRIPTURE

Jonah 1:1–2:10

SUPPLIES

Bible; one blanket; one action figure or doll; and one large, clean trash can

PREPARATION

Summarize Jonah 1:1–2:10. Say: **God told Jonah to deliver an important message to the people of Ninevah, but Jonah was scared. So instead, he tried to hide from God. He got on a ship and tried to go somewhere God wouldn't find him. But a huge storm came up, and the others on the ship figured out that Jonah had disobeyed God and that's why the storm was so fierce. So they threw him overboard. There in the water, a big fish swallowed him. Jonah was inside the fish's belly for three days. He prayed to God and asked for forgiveness for not following God's command. Then the fish spat him out on the beach, and Jonah went and delivered God's message to Ninevah.**

Help children form a circle around the blanket. Place the trash can in the center of the room where kids have an unobstructed view of the trash can. The group should be at least six to eight feet away from the trash can.

Say: **Imagine that your blanket is the sea, your action figure** [or doll] **is Jonah, and the trash can is the mouth of the big fish. You'll use your blanket to get Jonah into the trash can—without getting any closer to it.**

Encourage kids to work together to try to launch their action figure or doll into the trash can using the blanket (this will probably work best if the blanket is folded once so it's not too big). Kids may take as many turns as time allows.

Say: **Be careful not to hit anyone with your "Jonah."**

Debrief

After the game, congratulate kids on their efforts and discuss the following.

- *Describe what you think it would be like to be in the belly of a fish.*
- *Why do we sometimes resist God?*

• *Why is it important to obey God even when we're afraid of what he's asking?*

Say: **Jonah didn't want to obey God, but after he spent three nights in the belly of the great fish, he realized that he had to listen to God. God wants us to know that obeying him is always right—even when we are afraid—because he'll be there for us.**

Best for

AGES 6-9

Wash Tag

Kids try to avoid letting someone else
wash their feet.

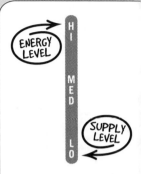

ENERGY LEVEL — HI MED LO

SUPPLY LEVEL

SUPPLIES

box of baby wipes

PREPARATION

Ask kids to take off their shoes and socks and set them aside. Girls wearing tights may still play, but caution them to be careful not to slip. Have the children sit in a circle on the floor.

Say: **Peter didn't want Jesus to wash his feet. He thought that Jesus was too special to serve him in that way. Let's play a game to act like Peter.**

Help kids find partners. Say: **Face each other so your fingers just barely touch with your arms outstretched in front of you.** Give each child a baby wipe. **Your goal is to tag your partner's feet with the baby wipe, without your partner tagging you and without moving from where you're standing. To keep the game safe, kicking is not allowed.**

If you have limited space, have the children play two at a time. Play for a minute, and then have the children find new partners. Play several rounds. If you have an uneven number of children, ensure that the group of three consists of different children each round.

Debrief

At the end of the game, discuss the following.

- *Explain what strategies you used to keep your partner from wiping your feet.*
- *What do you think is important about washing someone's feet?*
- *What example does Jesus set for us about serving others through his actions?*

Say: **Jesus taught his disciples an important lesson. He served others even though he was the most important person in the room. If he was willing to serve others, we can be happy to serve others as well.**

AGES 6-9

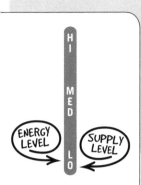

Best for

Words of Wisdom

This icebreaker helps kids appreciate the wisdom of God and their parents!

SCRIPTURE
Proverbs 2:2-4

SUPPLIES
Bible

PREPARATION
none

Have kids form groups of up to four.

Say: **Let's play a game that'll help us get to know each other better. I want you to introduce yourself to your group. Tell your name plus something wise you've learned from your parents.** Give them examples such as, "I'm Mrs. Black, and my mother told me to always turn off the hot water first when I finish filling the bathtub."

Say: **Listen carefully because you'll need to remember your friends' names and the wisdom they shared.** Explain that all the groups will come back together and introduce their group members to the entire group.

When everyone comes back together, give an example of an introduction such as, "This is my friend John. His father told him not to skate around parked cars." Have the child whose birthday is closest to today give the first introduction, then go around the circle. Continue until everyone has been introduced.

Debrief

At the end of the game, read aloud Proverbs 2:2-4. Discuss the following.

- *What does it mean to "tune your ears to wisdom"?*
- *Describe some wisdom you just learned from others in the group.*
- *Describe a person in your life whom you can go to for wisdom.*
- *Why do you think it's important to seek wisdom?*

Say: **People often need good advice to handle a problem or circumstance. Everyone needs wisdom. God wants us to seek wisdom so we make good choices and so we learn more about him.**

Communication

Best for

AGES 6-9

No Babble Babel

kids experiment with creative, non-verbal communication as they build a tower.

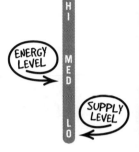
ENERGY LEVEL
SUPPLY LEVEL
HI MED LO

Point out your large supply of blocks. Ask: **If we were to build a tower with these blocks, how tall do you think we could go?** Encourage kids to offer guesses, then say: **Let's work together to build a tower, but let's do it in total silence!**

Explain that no one may talk or communicate in any way—including gestures. Set the timer for three minutes. When time is up, help kids estimate the tower's height.

Say: **Let's build it again, and this time one person will communicate through gestures.** Help kids decide who'll gesture. Set the timer for three minutes. Then build your tower and estimate its height when time is up.

Finish the game with a final round.

Say: **Let's build one last tower. This time anyone may gesture—but still no talking! After three minutes, we'll estimate the height.** Set the timer for three minutes. When time is up, help kids estimate the height.

SCRIPTURE

Genesis 11:4-7

SUPPLIES

Bible, timer or stopwatch, large tub of building blocks (any sort of stackable blocks will work, just be sure to have lots of them)

PREPARATION

After you've finished, bring kids together and read aloud Genesis 11:4-7. Then ask:

Debrief

- *Explain what it was like to work together without talking.*
- *In what ways did people's gestures make your task easier or more confusing?*
- *How was this experience like or unlike what happened when God confused everyone's words so they couldn't understand each other?*

Best for

AGES 6-9

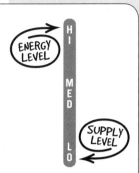
ENERGY LEVEL
HI
MED
LO
SUPPLY LEVEL

SCRIPTURE

1 Peter 2:4-5

SUPPLIES

Bible, masking tape

PREPARATION

Use the masking tape to mark two parallel starting lines on the floor at least 30 feet apart. Make a masking-tape "X" halfway between the two lines.

TIP If you're playing this game at an over-nighter or retreat, have kids use their rolled-up sleeping bags as stones rather than their shoes.

Building the House

kids learn they must to work together to be the church.

Gather kids around you.

Say: **The Bible tells us that all of Jesus' friends are like living stones, and God wants us to work together to build a strong house. When God's friends join together and cooperate, we're like a special, strong building that God can use. Let's play a game that'll help us experience what this means.**

Form two work crews. Have each work crew line up behind one of the starting lines so the crews are facing each other. If you have an extra-large group, simply add more work crews. You can have work crews approach the wall from all directions. The more the merrier!

Say: **Your crews are going to work together to build one big wall out of shoes. When I say "Go!" the first person in each line will run to the "X," take off his or her shoes, and place them on the "X." When the first person gets back behind the tape line, the next person in the work crew can add his or her shoes to the pile to help build the wall. You'll have to work together to make the pile of shoes look something like a wall.**

Shout "Go!" and let the children start building. Play until all kids have had a turn and no shoe remain.

· (Debrief) · ·

At the end of the game, read aloud 1 Peter 2:4-5. Then discuss the following.

- *Explain what was challenging about building this wall.*
- *How was working together on the wall like working together to build God's family?*
- *Why do you think it's important to God that we work together?*

Say: **God wants us to work together to be the church. He wants us to work close to each other—like stones built together in a wall. One of the great things about God's plan is that we get to work with other people and make great new friends.**

AGES 6-9

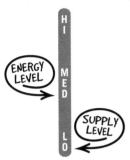

ENERGY LEVEL

SUPPLY LEVEL

H I M E D L O

SCRIPTURE

Luke 6:27-38

SUPPLIES

Bible, masking tape

PREPARATION

Create start and finish lines with masking tape on opposite sides of the playing area.

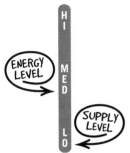

Hot Lava

Kids work together as a team and practice growing friendships.

Gather kids into groups of five.

Say: **The goal of this game is to work together as a team to get your group from start to finish across the "hot lava" floor—while making only 18 points of contact with the floor throughout your journey to the finish line.** Explain that every person in the group counts toward the total number of contact points with the floor. Kids can use toes, elbows, or any other part of their body as a contact point.

Once teams make it across the hot lava, say: **Great job. Now return to the start and try it again, this time only making 17 points of contact with the floor** (or one less than what it took them to complete the course). **Remember, you can lean on your teammates to help keep balance.**

Continue reducing points of contact until groups can no longer make it across without falling.

Debrief

At the end of the game, discuss the following.

* *Explain how you needed your teammates to play this game.*
* *How was this experience like or unlike what it means to have good friends?*
* *How can you help someone who doesn't have many friends?*

Read aloud Luke 6:27-38.

* *How can you be a friend to others like Jesus is a friend to you?*

Say: **Jesus tells us to love our enemies and treat others as we want to be treated. Jesus wants us to work together as friends. One thing friends do is help each other.**

AGES 6-9

Knock It Off!

Kids see that their value comes from God.

Philippians 2:3-5

Bible; one clean, balled-up sock for every pair of children

F orm pairs, give each pair a sock, and then choose one to be "It" first.

Say: **If you are It, you will begin the game by saying as many things you like about yourself as possible in one minute. Each time you say something good about yourself, you'll toss your sock straight up in the air and catch it to represent that good thing. For example, you could say, "I like that I can play the piano," and then toss your sock up and catch it. Your partner's goal will be to try to snatch away the sock before you can catch it.**

Play for one minute, then have kids switch roles. Play for an even number of turns, and then call time and collect the socks.

After the game, discuss:

- *Describe how it felt to say things you like about yourself.*
- *What was it like to have your sock snatched away after saying something good about yourself?*
- *How did it feel to snatch away someone else's sock?*
- *How was this game like what happens when we put each other down?*

Read aloud Philippians 2:3-5.

- *What does the Bible tell us about how God wants us to treat each other?*
- *What's one thing you can do to remember what you like about yourself when someone else puts you down?*

Say: **God values each and every one of us. When others feel bad or get discouraged, we can show them God values them.** Have kids pat a friend's back and say, "You're awesome!"

AGES 6-9

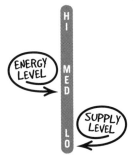

Lifelines

Kids see that Jesus is our rescuer who offers us a lifeline when we're trapped in sin.

John 3:16-17

Bible, one jump rope for every four kids

Form groups of four. Give one child in each group a jump rope. Those kids will be the "Rescuers."

Say: **Often when a person is trapped somewhere and can't get out, rescuers throw the person a lifeline to hold onto while the person is pulled to safety. In this game, the jump ropes will be the lifelines.**

Have Rescuers stand on one side of the room while the other kids mingle around at the opposite end of the room until they are no longer in groups.

Say: **Everyone except the Rescuers, kneel and close your eyes. At my signal, everyone but the Rescuers will keep your eyes closed and silently raise your hands. When I say "Go!" Rescuers will speed walk to their group members and rescue them one by one. To rescue a group member, the Rescuer will tap the person on the shoulder, then help the person stand up and hold the lifeline. Then the Rescuer will usher the rescued person across the room to the safety zone. You can open your eyes only when you've reached the safety zone.**

As time permits, play several rounds, having kids change groups and roles. This game is best played in a large room or outdoors. If you're indoors, remove all obstacles from the center of the room.

At the end of the game, read aloud John 3:16-17. Discuss the following.

- *Describe what it was like waiting to be rescued.*
- *Explain what it was like when the Rescuer came for you.*
- *How is being saved from our sins by Jesus like being thrown a lifeline?*

Say: **Just as trapped people need a lifeline to rescue them, sin traps all of us and we all need Jesus to save us. Jesus is our Rescuer, our Savior who throws us the lifeline of forgiveness and eternal life.**

AGES 6-9

Save the Sock

Kids discover how Jesus has
come to save all of us.

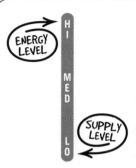

SCRIPTURE

Psalm 73:26

SUPPLIES

Bible, one clean sock for
every five kids

PREPARATION

Let kids choose groups of five and form a circle. (If you have fewer than 10 kids, just form one circle.) Have one child from each group take a sock and hang it on the front of his or her shirt like a bib. Make sure the sock can be pulled away easily. Choose one child from each group to stand outside the circle.

Say: **The goal of this game is for the child outside the circle to nab the sock. Kids in the circle can keep the sock out of reach by turning individually and rotating the circle itself, but they can't cover the sock with their hands.**

Once the child outside the circle grabs the sock, have kids switch roles and play again.

Debrief

At the end of the game, discuss the following.

- *What was it like to try to save the sock?*
- *Explain whether you were tempted to give up.*
- *Tell about a time you gave up on something—maybe something like studying for a test or winning at a sport.*

Read aloud Psalm 73:26.

- *Why can we put our trust in God when we feel like giving up?*

Say: **The Bible tells us that God gives us strength. We can rely on him when we feel weak and want to give up.**

Best for

AGES 6-9

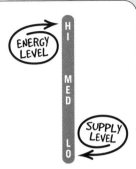

SCRIPTURE

Acts 27:1-44

SUPPLIES

Bible, misting fan bottle (optional)

PREPARATION

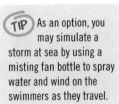

TIP As an option, you may simulate a storm at sea by using a misting fan bottle to spray water and wind on the swimmers as they travel.

Shipwreck Unrace

Kids practice looking out for others, encouraging others, and reaching a common goal.

Designate one area in the room to be the shipwreck and another area to be the island.

Say: **The goal is for everyone to "swim" to the island, but you can only arrive safely if everyone touches the island at the same time. The trick of the game is to keep an eye on everyone else and encourage each other along.**

Assign each player a different swimming style to do as they "swim" from the shipwreck to the island. Swimming styles you assign might include backstroke, sidestroke, dog paddle, tiptoeing (to keep head above water), crab-walking (along the bottom), sliding feet through the mud, whirlpool swimming (spinning), bouncing up and down on waves, riptide (two steps forward and one step back), and so on. When everyone knows his or her "stroke," show swimmers the path they must swim, which might include a couple of trips around the room's furniture before reaching the island. Then give the signal to begin.

When the fastest swimmers approach the island, remind them to think of ways to help or encourage slower swimmers as they "tread water" and wait.

If anyone touches the island early, say: **A wave has washed you back to sea. Look for another swimmer to swim next to. You can keep using the same stroke, but adjust it to match the slower swimmer's pace.** Encourage kids to wait for everyone else. After a few attempts, designate a signal to indicate that all swimmers are ready to touch the island.

When all the swimmers have gathered around the island, signal them to touch it together and then cheer for safe arrival.

At the end of the game, discuss the following.

- *What made this game easier or more difficult?*

Read aloud Acts 27:1-44.

- *What do you think about Paul's constant encouragement to his shipmates when they were in trouble?*
- *What difference does it make when others help or encourage you when you're doing something difficult or scary?*

Challenge your kids to think of ways they can be encouragers at their school, in the church, and for their family.

AGES 6-9

SUPPLIES

10 pennies

PREPARATION

Trust Me

Kids discover that they can't always trust others but they can always trust Jesus.

Ask a willing child to stack the pennies on an upside-down elbow, as shown.

Say: **Will you try to catch those pennies without using your other hand? To catch pennies, turn your raised hand up, drop your elbow quickly, and scoop up the pennies before they fall.** Demonstrate this as needed.

Before the child attempts the catch, say: **Try to predict how many pennies you can catch on one try. Tell everyone, "I can catch** [number] **pennies. Trust me."**

Allow the other kids to say whether they trust the predictions.

Give kids three tries each to make their predictions come true. Then have them pass the pennies to another child. Play until each child has had a turn.

Debrief

At the end of the game, discuss the following.

- *What helped you decide whether you trusted someone's prediction?*
- *Tell about a time you trusted someone and were disappointed.*
- *How do you know you can trust Jesus?*

Say: **People don't always keep their promises. But we can always trust Jesus because he keeps his promises and loves each of us.**

Best for

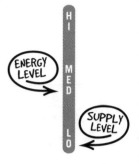

AGES 6-9

Levelheaded

kids try not to put themselves above others.

SCRIPTURE

Matthew 18:1-5

Open your Bible to Matthew 18:1-5, and read aloud or summarize what Jesus said about entering God's kingdom.

Ask:

• *What does it mean to be humble?*

Say: **To be humble means not to put yourself above anyone else. Who wants to tell about a time when it was difficult for you to be humble?** Allow time for kids to respond.

Say: **Sometimes it's tough to be humble. But practice will help us remember this, so let's play a game to practice not putting ourselves above others.**

Choose a child to be the Leveler, and line up the rest of the kids behind him or her. Have kids position themselves so their heads are level with the heads of the children in front of them. The object of the game is for kids to stay in line and keep their heads level with those in front of them.

Ask the Leveler to walk around the room and change the position of his or her head (up and down, side to side, and so on). The Leveler can change the speed, direction, and method of travel, too. He or she can jog, hop, and even go under tables! Play several rounds with a new Leveler each time.

SUPPLIES

Bible

PREPARATION

· Debrief · ·

After the game, discuss the following.

• *Explain whether it was easy or difficult to stay level with the people in front of you.*
• *How is this experience like not putting yourself above others in real life?*

Say: **Jesus wants us to be humble. This week, practice putting others above yourself.**

Best for

AGES 6-9

ENERGY LEVEL   SUPPLY LEVEL

HI MED LO

SCRIPTURE

Philippians 2:14-15

SUPPLIES

Bible, ball of yarn

PREPARATION

Point of Light

Kids learn that teamwork allows them to create something beautiful.

Form a circle.

Say: **Although we're special as individuals, God has also called us to be united in Jesus. I'll start by holding this end of the yarn, and tossing the ball of yarn to someone else in the group. As I do, I'll say something positive about the person I'm tossing the ball of yarn to.**

Hold on to the end of the yarn and toss the yarn ball to someone across the circle. Say: **My name is _____ and what I like about** [the person's name] **is _____.**

Have each child hold his or her bit of yarn and then toss the ball to someone else (not the people directly beside the child), saying something good about that person.

When everyone has had a turn to catch the yarn and pass it to someone else, say: **Together, we're a wondrously beautiful creation of God. Look at the beautiful star we made!**

Show kids the formation created by the yarn.

Say: **It wasn't hard, and all it took was a little encouragement and working together.**

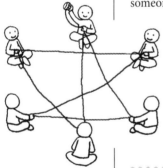

Debrief

After the game, discuss the following.

- *Describe what it was like to hear people say nice things about you.*
- *Why is it important for us to work together as Christians?*

Read aloud Philippians 2:14-15. Then ask:

- *What are ways you can shine bright for Jesus?*
- *What are some beautiful things we could do together to make Jesus smile?*

Cooperation

Jump the Jordan

Facing a challenge, kids work together and look for ways to help one another.

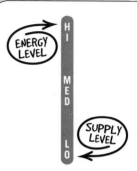

SCRIPTURE

Joshua 3:1, 14-17

SUPPLIES

Bible, two long ropes

PREPARATION

Stretch out the two ropes across the floor of your game area, parallel to each other and a few inches apart.

Ask a willing child to read aloud Joshua 3:1, 14-17. Then point to the ropes and tell kids that they represent the Jordan River. Arrange kids so they're all standing on one "shore." At your signal, they will all jump across the "river," being careful not to get their toes "wet" by touching the space between the ropes. Widen the river by moving the ropes a couple of inches further apart. Have all the kids jump back over to the first side. Continue to widen the river, a little at a time, after each jump.

When the ropes are finally far enough apart that jumping across is a challenge, explain what'll happen when someone "falls in." Any child whose foot touches between the ropes has to stay in the river until rescued. Kids on the shore may become "Life Preservers" by stretching out a hand to the child stuck in the river. If the child is too far away to reach, encourage the group to figure out how to become a lifesaver chain, perhaps by holding hands or linking arms in the river to reach the stranded child. Have everyone stop jumping until the child is rescued.

Continue to gradually widen the ropes as long as any child is interested in continuing to try to jump the river. The kids who choose to stay on the shore can look for opportunities to be Life Preservers and pull out anyone who doesn't make it. Play until no one can jump as wide as the river and everyone's safely on a shore.

> **TIP** You may want to assign one child to stay at the opposite end of the ropes from you and help you move them to keep the game fast-paced.

Debrief

At the end of the game, discuss the following.

- *What did you like about using teamwork to cross the river today?*
- *The people of Israel walked across the river on dry ground. How do you think they might've helped each other as they crossed?*
- *In what ways can we help others—here at church and in other places?*

Best for

AGES 6-9

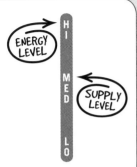

ENERGY LEVEL

SUPPLY LEVEL

HI

MED

LO

SUPPLIES

Bible, five foam footballs or other soft balls, masking tape

PREPARATION

Create a centerline across the room with masking tape.

Team Powerball

kids play a game that turns two teams into one big team.

Form two teams, and tell kids they can't cross the centerline unless they're joining the other team. Toss the balls to one team.

Say: **The goal is to toss the balls so they touch a child on the other team before touching the ground. If you tag someone, he or she immediately joins your team. Try to intercept the balls and use them to grow your team by tagging more kids.**

Play until all players are on one team, then declare everyone winners.

Debrief

At the end of the game, discuss the following.

- *What did you think about going to join the other team or having new people come to your team?*
- *Why do you think we all won in this game?*
- *How is playing this game like living for God?*

Say: **When we live for God, we're on a winning team. And best of all, God's team has room for everyone.**

AGES 6-9

A Hill of Beans

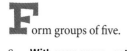

Kids discover during this "hill-of-beans" game how lies destroy trust.

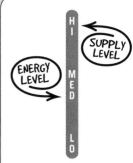

Form groups of five.

Say: **With your group, gather around one of the tablecloths on the floor. That area will serve as your team's workspace. I'm going to give each group a pound of each type of bean.**

As kids put on food-service gloves, say: **Each time we talk, we can choose to tell the truth or to tell a lie. When people tell a lot of lies, we may say their words aren't "worth a hill of beans." Right now, you're going to work with your team to build the tallest hill of beans.**

Give teams three minutes. When time's up, have kids gather all their beans and fill the large resealable bags. Attach the recipe, found after the game, to the bag for kids to donate to a local food shelter.

Debrief

Afterward, read aloud Proverbs 12:22 and Ephesians 4:24-25.

Then discuss the following.

- *What happened when you tried to build a hill of beans?*
- *How was this experience like or unlike what happens when lies pile up?*
- *How do lies ruin people's trust?*
- *What kinds of things happen when we tell the truth, even when it's not easy?*

Say: **God wants us to tell the truth. Let's ask God to help us always be honest and trustworthy at school, church, and home.** Close in prayer, asking God to help kids remember how important the truth is. Also, ask him to bless the recipients of the soup mix bags.

SCRIPTURE

Proverbs 12:22;
Ephesians 4:24-25

SUPPLIES

Bible, gallon-size resealable plastic bags, food-service gloves, plastic tablecloths, one pound of each of the following for each group of five: black beans, red kidney beans, pinto beans, Great Northern beans, navy beans, lentils, yellow split peas, green split peas, and black-eyed peas.

PREPARATION

Spread tablecloths to serve as each team's workspace. Make copies of the recipe to attach to the soup mixes.

Nine Bean Soup
Yields 8 to 10 cups or 8 servings

Add to this package of Nine Bean Soup Mix:
8 cups cold water
1/2 teaspoon salt
1 pound ham, diced (optional)
1 large onion, cleaned and chopped
1 clove garlic, minced or 1/2 teaspoon dry garlic
1 16-ounce can diced tomatoes
1 10-ounce can tomatoes and green chilies

• Sort and wash bean mix. Place in a bowl, fill to 2 inches above
  the beans with cold water, cover and soak overnight.
• Drain beans; add water, ham, onion, garlic and salt. Simmer until
  navy beans (smallest white bean) are tender, 1½ to 2 hours.
• Add tomatoes and chilies and simmer 30 minutes to blend
  flavors. Stir occasionally. Serve hot.

School Pressure

AGES 6-9

Belly Ball

Kids bounce a ball off their bellies and explore conflict.

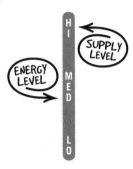

SCRIPTURE

Titus 3:1-2

SUPPLIES

Bible; two beach balls; masking tape; a large, clean trash can; one index card per child; pens or pencils

PREPARATION

Using masking tape, create a line on the floor for kids to stand behind. Place a large, clean trash can several feet past this line.

orm two teams.

Say: **When I say "Go!" each player will stand behind the line and try to make a basket in the trash can by bouncing the beach ball off his or her belly. The team with the most baskets will win.**

After teams have played the game once, say: **Let's play again. This time, the team on the right of the basket can shoot normally while the team on the left continues bouncing the ball off their stomachs to make a basket.**

Afterward, gather all the kids around and put the beach balls somewhere out of sight to avoid distraction.

Debrief

At the end of the game, discuss the following.

- *Describe what you were thinking when I gave one team permission to use their hands to make a basket.*
- *How was this game fair or unfair?*
- *How do you handle unfair situations in life?*

Read aloud Titus 3:1-2.

- *The next time you face a conflict, how can this verse help you remember how to handle it?*

Have kids write or draw a personal reminder of today's lesson on an index card that they can take to school and keep somewhere to help them remember what they learned about conflict. Talk about situations at school that might be difficult or unfair and how God wants kids to handle those situations.

Play the game again, and let the other team play normally while the opposite team bounces the ball off their bellies.

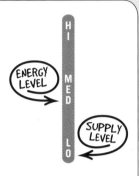

AGES 6-9

ENERGY LEVEL

SUPPLY LEVEL

SCRIPTURE

1 Corinthians 12:12-26

SUPPLIES

Bible

PREPARATION

TIP This is an excellent game to involve kids with special needs. You'll need a large room for this experience.

Bridging the Gap

Kids discover that God made everyone unique, and everyone is important.

The object of this game is for kids to connect in such a way as to be able to touch two walls of a gymnasium or large room at the same time.

Say: **One person starts by touching a wall with a body part like a hand, foot, or elbow. The rest of you must connect to each other to reach to the opposite wall. Every person has to be involved, and you can get creative on how to reach the other side of the room.** If your room is small, have kids extend in one chain across the room and back to the starting wall.

Your role in this challenge is that of a guide. Once you've given directions, sit back and watch to see how kids respond. If five minutes pass without any progress made, give kids hints as to how to accomplish the task. Only give directions in small doses. Let kids try to figure this out on their own as much as possible.

If kids get stuck, you may say: **You don't have to be physically touching each other. You can use sweaters, shoelaces, jackets, socks, or whatever else you can find to help bridge the gaps as long you're still connected.** Allow kids time to figure out their strategy, and only give hints if they're really stumped.

Debrief

At the end of the game, discuss the following.

- *What were you thinking when I first gave you this challenge?*
- *Explain what was helpful as you tried to accomplish the goal.*
- *Why was everyone important in this game?*

Say: **For this challenge, everybody was equally important. Everyone made it possible to achieve the goal. God wants us to work together to solve problems and find solutions— and everyone has important contributions to make.**

Best for

AGES 6-9

Candle Tag

Kids remember to be lights for Jesus.

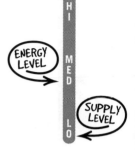

ENERGY LEVEL

SUPPLY LEVEL

SCRIPTURE

Matthew 5:14-16

SUPPLIES

Bible, one flameless tea light for each child

PREPARATION

Find an open space that you can darken (but not totally black out). Ask for an adult volunteer to help you with this game.

Say: **I'm going to give you each a candle. For now, keep the light turned off. I need someone who's willing to be "It."**

Turn off the lights in the room. Ask an adult volunteer to stand in the center of the room with a tea light turned on to serve as Base.

Say: **The child who's It will sneak in the darkness to tag the other kids. You can stay safe at Base until you count to five, but then you have to move away from Base and into the darkness. When It tags you, turn on your light and join the Base.**

Once everyone's tagged, play more rounds with a new It.

Afterward, read aloud Matthew 5:14-16.

Debrief

At the end of the game, discuss the following.

• *What was good about joining Base when you got tagged? when you needed to stay safe?*
• *In what way was this experience like or unlike how we shine our light for God?*
• *What's one thing you can do this week to shine your light in your community or school?*

Say: **God wants us to be lights in the darkness and share what we know about Jesus with others. Let's be a bright light in our community so others can see Jesus.**

AGES 6-9

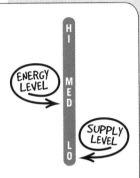

SCRIPTURE

Acts 14:21-22;
2 Corinthians 11:23-28

SUPPLIES

Bible

PREPARATION

Human Obstacle Course

Kids measure their smiles and spread their joy

Say: **Let's brainstorm ways that a pair of kids could become an obstacle. For example, one pair could become an archway to walk under by pressing hands together up high. Other pairs could become a swinging gate to push through by stretching out arms, logs to step over by lying on the floor, or soldiers to duck past by swinging arms like swords.** After brainstorming, form pairs and let each pair choose a different obstacle to become.

Once all the pairs have figured out their obstacles, spread them out in a circular path around the room. Say: **Now, we'll have one pair at a time leave their spot to walk through the obstacle course. When they've completed the course, they will return to their spot to become an obstacle again, and another pair will get a turn.** Encourage partners to look for ways to help each other through the obstacles. Play until all have had a turn to travel through the obstacle course.

Say: **The Bible shows us that Paul went through many obstacles on his way to telling others about Jesus.** Read aloud Acts 14:21-22 and 2 Corinthians 11:23-28.

Debrief

At the end of the game, discuss the following.

* *Explain what it was like to work through all these obstacles.*
* *Why do you think Paul kept going even when he faced huge obstacles?*
* *What are ways we can help each other through obstacles in our lives?*

Say: **Spreading the word about Jesus isn't always easy—sometimes we face obstacles. But we can work together to help each other though those obstacles.**

Conflict

AGES 6-9

Sock It to Me

Kids discover that God protects us all the time, and especially when we need help.

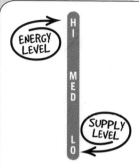

SCRIPTURE

Psalm 91:14-15

SUPPLIES

Bible

PREPARATION

Say: **Sit in a tight circle and remove your shoes. I'm going to choose two kids to be "It." They'll sit on their knees in the center of the circle. The rest of you in the circle must stay seated with your feet in the center of the circle.**

Once kids are in position, say: **The object of the game is for the It Pair to take the rest of your socks before the kids who are sitting in the circle can take the It Pair's socks.**

Remind children to be careful when playing so they don't accidentally kick a neighbor.

Once the It team wins, let two different kids be It. Continue playing as time allows.

Afterward, discuss the following.

- *What was your strategy for keeping your socks protected and for taking others' socks?*
- *How was this experience like or unlike what happens when trouble comes in real life?*

Read aloud Psalm 91:14-15

- *The Bible tells us that God is with us all the time, but especially during troubled times. Describe a time when you needed God's help.*
- *How can we remember to rely on God when trouble comes?*

Say: **Sometimes we can feel under attack, like nothing is going right. During those times, God especially wants us to rely on him and trust him with our worries, fears, and frustrations.**

Best for

AGES 6-9

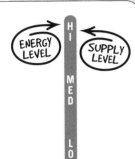

ENERGY LEVEL / SUPPLY LEVEL

HI MED LO

SCRIPTURE

Isaiah 30:18-19

SUPPLIES

Bible, two combination locks, candy (at least one piece per child), timer or stopwatch, two colored dot stickers with matching paper

PREPARATION

Before kids arrive, place one dot sticker on the back of each lock. Hide the locks in the room. Print the corresponding combination numbers out of sequence on the lock's matching paper, but keep both correct combinations with you.

ALLERGY ALERT!
See page 8

Unlocked

Kids learn the importance of being patient and listening for God's instructions.

Say: **We're going to play a game where teams race to open locks that I've hidden in this room. We'll form two teams, and I'm going to give each team the combination numbers that'll open their respective locks. Your teams will race each other to find their corresponding lock and figure out the correct combination. The first team to return with an open lock will get a reward. The numbers are scrambled and you must guess the correct sequence. We'll form our teams based on which one of two strategies you want to use:**

1. On "Go!" Team One will race to find its lock. Once they find the lock, they have to work together to decipher the correct combination using the scrambled numbers on the paper.

2. On "Go!" Team Two will delay their search for 30 seconds (giving the other team a head start), but I'll give them the correct combination to their lock. That way, all they have to do is find the lock and open it.

Have kids form two teams based on which strategy they believe will work. It's okay if teams are uneven. Give the signal to start. No matter which team returns with an open lock first, reward everyone for their efforts with candy. As kids enjoy their treat, read aloud Isaiah 30:18-19.

Debrief

At the end of the game, discuss the following.

- *Tell how well your team's strategy worked.*
- *Why did you choose that strategy?*
- *How was this experience like or unlike being patient and listening for God's instructions?*

Say: **Just like it's important to listen to instructions from our parents and teachers, it's really important to listen to God for instructions on what's happening in our lives.**

AGES 6-9

Who's Molding You?

Kids see the importance of letting
God shape their lives.

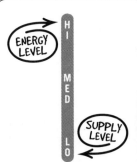

Isaiah 64:8

Bible, clay

Have kids form groups of four. Give each group a lump of clay.
Say: **The Bible talks about God being the potter and us being the clay. In
your groups, work together to mold your clay into a symbol representing
what you think God would want you to be.**

After kids have made their objects, line up the groups in relay teams
with kids standing at least 10 feet apart. Designate how many laps the
teams will do. Have groups run a circular relay (like running around an
oval track), using their group's clay object as a baton. Each person can
pass off the baton to a new teammate upon reaching the starting
line. Play until all players have carried the baton.

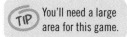

You'll need a large
area for this game.

Gather kids and discuss the following.

- *Describe what happened to your group's clay symbol
  when you used it as a baton.*
- *The Bible tells us that God will mold us. How is the way we handled the
  clay during our relay like what happens when we try to mold ourselves?*
- *What people or things are influencing your life?*
- *What's some way you need God to mold you?*

Say: **You might face pressure at school from people wanting you to
make bad decisions. Remember to let God mold you, instead of allowing others to mold you.**

AGES 6-9

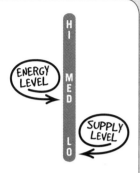

ENERGY LEVEL

SUPPLY LEVEL

SCRIPTURE

Proverbs 19:8-9

SUPPLIES

Bible, ball of yarn

PREPARATION

Tangled Web

Kids will discover how lies can entangle us.

Say: **Lies are sticky like glue. When we tell a lie, often we end up having to tell other lies to cover for the first lie. Let's play a game to see how lies can trap us.**

Have kids form a circle. Starting with yourself, toss the ball of yarn around the circle.

Say: **When each person gets the yarn, he or she will give an example of a common lie, such as "My dog ate my homework," and wrap the yarn around his or her body somehow. Don't wrap the yarn around your neck.**

Once the yarn web has everyone wrapped up, say: **On "Go!" everyone try to get untangled as quickly as possible.**

Once everyone is freed, collect the yarn and have kids sit. Read aloud (or have a willing child read aloud) Proverbs 19:8-9.

Debrief

At the end of the game, discuss the following.

- *What made getting untangled difficult or easy for you?*
- *How is being tangled in the yarn like or unlike what happens when we tell lies?*
- *How can we avoid getting tangled in lies?*
- *Why does it matter if we're honest?*

To end in prayer, say: **Dear God, thank you for helping us be honest. Please help us remember how harmful lies are when we're faced with a situation where it might be easy to lie. In Jesus' name, amen.**

Self-Image

Distinctly Designed

Kids see the importance of letting God shape their lives.

AGES 6-9

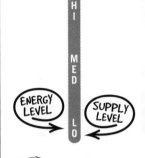

 SCRIPTURE

Psalm 139:13-16

 SUPPLIES

Bible

 PREPARATION

Ask everyone to sit in a circle on the floor. If your group is larger than 20, form more than one circle. Choose one person to be the "Answer Person." Everyone else will hide his or her eyes. Instruct the Answer Person to walk around the outside of the circle, tapping everyone on the back once except for one person, whom he or she will tap twice. Then have the Answer Person sit down in the middle of the circle and announce that everyone can uncover their eyes.

Say: **One of you got tapped twice on the back rather than just once. You're our Mystery Person—don't tell anyone! The goal of this game is to identify the Mystery Person by asking the Answer Person in the middle yes-or-no questions, such as "Does the Mystery Person have brown hair?" "Does the Mystery Person like volleyball?" and so on. If you're the Mystery Person, you can participate in asking questions also so you don't reveal who you are by not participating.**

Let everyone in the circle take turns asking questions until there's a group consensus on who the Mystery Person is. Play several rounds, so everyone has a chance to be the Answer Person or the Mystery Person.

Afterward, read aloud Psalm 139:13-16.

At the end of the game, discuss the following.

- *What made it easy or difficult to find the Mystery Person?*
- *What are some key characteristics that distinguished one person from another?*
- *What does this Scripture tell you about your uniqueness?*

Say: **God gave each of us different characteristics and qualities. That means he made each of us uniquely special. He doesn't want us to try to be like someone else—he wants us to be us just how he made us!**

Best for

AGES 6-9

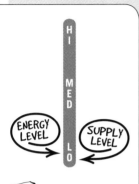

SCRIPTURE

1 John 5:14-15

SUPPLIES

Bible

PREPARATION

Listen Hard

Kids learn to listen as they think about prayer.

Have all the kids sit in a circle. Ask for a willing child to stand in the center of the circle, close his or her eyes, and listen very carefully.

Say: **When I clap my hands, everyone sitting in the circle will say a number between 100 and 150—all at the same time.**

Clap your hands and let kids say their numbers. Then ask the child in the middle to repeat what everyone in the circle said. To make listening difficult, make sure kids respond at the same time.

Switch roles, and ask for the responses to the following categories, or substitute your own.

- a letter of the alphabet
- a favorite color
- the streets they live on
- a nonsense word
- the name of a foreign country
- their shoe sizes

After everyone gets a chance to be in the middle, read aloud 1 John 5:14-15.

Debrief

At the end of the game, discuss the following.

- *How easy or difficult was it to listen to everyone at once?*
- *How hard do you think it is for God to listen to everyone's prayers at the same time? Why?*
- *Why do you think God tells us to pray to him?*

Say: **Even though we don't know how he does it, God answers all our prayers, in his own way, in his own time. And he always listens to us.**

AGES 6-9

Pool Noodle Freeze Tag

Kids discover that God answers prayers and helps us.

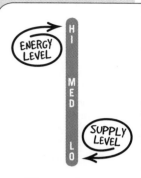

Say: **The Bible tells us we can call out to God for help when we need it. Let's play a game to remind us of that.**

Select a willing child to be the "Tagger" and use a pool noodle to attempt to tag the others. Choose another child to be the "Unfreezer" for the tagged kids. If you have more than 20 kids playing together, consider adding a second Tagger with another pool noodle.

Say: **If you're tagged with the noodle, call out for help. When the Unfreezer responds to your call by tagging you, you can rejoin the game.**

After a few minutes, allow other kids to take over the role of Tagger and Unfreezer.

End the game by calling kids to you and reading aloud Psalm 34:17-18.

SCRIPTURE
Psalm 34:17-18

SUPPLIES
Bible, one or two pool noodles

PREPARATION
none

Debrief

At the end of the game, discuss the following.

- *Explain what was easy or difficult about this game.*
- *What were you thinking when you got tagged? brought back into the action by a friend?*
- *How is this experience like being in a difficult situation and praying for help?*
- *Why do you think God wants to help us when we cry out for help?*

Say: **In this game, it was easy to answer a cry for help. In real life, we can go to God with our biggest problems. We can be thankful—and take comfort—knowing that God answers our prayers for help**

Best for

AGES 6-9

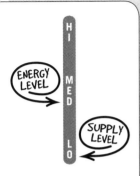

ENERGY LEVEL

SUPPLY LEVEL

SCRIPTURE

Luke 19:1-10

SUPPLIES

Bible, balloons

PREPARATION

Blow up and tie off at least 25 balloons before class.

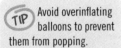

TIP Avoid overinflating balloons to prevent them from popping.

BALLOON WARNING!
See page 8

Static Shapes

Kids use balloons to change an animal's shape and discover how Jesus' love changes us.

Read aloud Luke 19:1-10.

Say: **From this passage we know that Jesus' love changes us. Let's play a game about changing!**

Have kids form groups of four. Say: **In this game, each group will arrange balloons on a wall in the shape of an animal. Each group's animal must be different from the previous group's animal.**

Have groups think of an animal and whisper it to you. Make sure no teams choose the same animals. Gather in front of a blank wall.

Say: **Let's rub the inflated balloons on our heads to create static electricity and then stick the balloons on the wall in no particular pattern.**

Once the balloons are in place, say: **Move to the opposite side of the room and get back into your groups.**

Let the first group run to the wall and move the balloons into their chosen animal shape. After one minute, say: **Time's up. Can anyone guess the animal?** (If kids can't guess, let the group name the animal.)

Let the next group change the balloons into a different animal, and so on, until all groups have had a turn. If balloons lose their static electricity, just have kids rub them on their heads again.

Debrief

At the end of the game, discuss the following.

- *Explain how each balloon animal was different from the others.*
- *Which was your favorite balloon animal, and why?*
- *How do you think coming in contact with Jesus changed Zacchaeus?*
- *In what ways has knowing Jesus changed your life?*

Close with a prayer thanking Jesus for his life-changing love.

AGES 6-9

Trashy Test

Kids experience being polluters and cleaners.

SCRIPTURE

Jeremiah 2:6-7

SUPPLIES

Bible, newspapers, trash bags

PREPARATION

Say: **As people, we tend to make a mess of God's beautiful world. Let's see what the Bible says about how God felt when people long ago didn't respect him or his creation.**

Read aloud Jeremiah 2:6-7.

Say: **Let's play a game to help us understand how God feels when he sees what a mess we've made of his beautiful creation.**

Help kids count off by threes. Invite the ones and twos to form a big circle. Give each child in the circle a piece of newspaper. Give each child in group three a trash bag. Have kids in group three get on their hands and knees in the middle of the circle.

Say: **On "Go!" players in groups one and two will tear their newspapers into little pieces and throw the pieces into the circle as quickly as possible. Members of group three will try to keep the circle clean by picking up all the paper and putting it in the bags.**

Call time after one minute, and see if group three kept the circle clean.

Afterward, have everyone gather the paper shreds and let another group try to keep the circle clean.

Debrief

At the end of the game, discuss the following.

- *What was easy or difficult about throwing all that garbage into the circle? about keeping the circle clean?*
- *How does our faith impact how we think about keeping the earth clean?*
- *What ways do you help care for God's earth? What else can you do to help care for the earth?*

Finish your time with a prayer, thanking God for his beautiful creation and asking him to help us remember to take care of it.

AGES 6-9

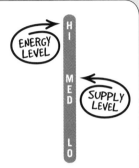

Defend the Faith

As kids try to defend themselves against paper wads, they'll discover that God helps us when it's tough to be a Christian.

SCRIPTURE

Acts 5:12-42

SUPPLIES

Bible, masking tape, lots of newspaper

PREPARATION

Place a masking-tape line across the center of the playing area, dividing the room into two equal spaces. Then put two parallel tape lines on the floor, perpendicular to the center line, about 3 feet from each edge of the playing area. These side areas will be out of bounds.

Form two teams of equal size, and place one team on each side of the playing area. Designate one group the "Apostles" and the other group the "Sadducees." Explain the boundaries, and give each group a pile of newspaper.

Open your Bible to Acts 5:12-42 and read the passage aloud.

Say: **We know from the Bible that the apostles had to stand up to the Sadducees and defend their faith. They taught and performed miracles in Jesus' name. Crowds came from all over to witness what they were doing. But the Sadducees were very jealous that the Apostles were getting so much attention. They had the Apostles thrown in jail. The Sadducees told the Apostles to stop teaching and performing miracles. But when they released the Apostles, they went right back into the Temple and taught again even though they were afraid. When the Sadducees confronted them, the Apostles said, "We must obey God rather than human authority." Now that takes courage!**

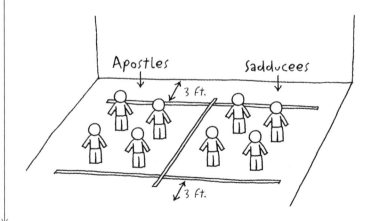

In this game, it'll be the Sadducees' job to throw paper wads at the Apostles, and it'll be the Apostles' job to hit the paper wads into out-of-bounds areas. Any paper wads that fall on the Sadducees' side of play but not out of bounds can be picked up and thrown again. Paper wads hit out of bounds can't be used again. The Apostles can use their newspaper however they want to hit away the paper wads. (They can make bats, shields, or golf clubs out of the newspaper.) **But they can't use their hands, only the newspaper.**

Allow a few minutes for kids to prepare by making paper wads or shields and bats. Play for about five minutes, and then have groups switch roles and play again. Ask kids to help you clean up between rounds and at the end of the game.

Debrief

Afterward, discuss the following.

- *Explain what it was like when you were fighting off the paper wads.*
- *How is that like having to defend your faith?*
- *What are some ways you can defend your faith in Jesus when people challenge you?*

Say: **Just as God gave the apostles strength to stand up for their faith, God helps us when it's difficult to be a Christian.**

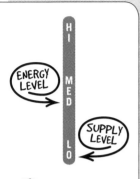

ENERGY
LEVEL

SUPPLY
LEVEL

SCRIPTURE

Exodus 14:13-14

SUPPLIES

Bible, blindfold

PREPARATION

Startled Steps

Kids get a surprise along their blindfolded path to courage.

Choose one person to be "It." Blindfold this person, and take It to one side of the room. Scatter the remaining players around the playing area.

When you say "Go!" the blindfolded player will slowly begin to move to the other side of the room while trying to touch the opposite wall while bumping into as few people as possible along the way.

Remaining players should stand silent and motionless. Whenever the blindfolded person bumps another player, the seeing player must shout "Hey!" Play continues until the blindfolded player has reached the other side of the room.

Ask It to give the blindfold to another player, then join the others as potential obstacles. Have kids take turns until everyone has had a chance to cross the room.

Debrief

At the end of the game, discuss the following.

• *Explain what it was like to be blindfolded and play this game.*
• *How was this game similar to challenges we face each day that make us uncertain or fearful?*

Read aloud Exodus 14:13-14; then ask:

• *What do you think this Scripture means?*
• *How can you stay calm and trust God to help you when you need it?*

Play the game again, having a sighted person walk alongside the blindfolded person repeating, "Be calm—God will protect you."

AGES 6-9

Creation Race

Kids go on a scavenger hunt to learn about the seven days of creation.

Open your Bible. Have kids take turns reading aloud Genesis 1:1-31; 2:1-3.

Say: **That's what happened when God created the earth. Let's play a fun game to explore this further.**

Form two teams, and designate a goal line. Give each team a copy of the seven-step instructions found after this game. Tell teams they'll race to complete the steps and that they'll have to find the supplies to complete each task. The teams must work together to find items for each step, with different kids completing each task. Encourage kids who are good readers to read each step aloud to their group.

 Debrief

After both teams are finished, discuss the following.

- *Describe what it was like to "create" so many things.*
- *What do you think it was like when God created everything?*
- *Why was everything that God made good?*

 SCRIPTURE

Genesis 1:1-31; 2:1-3

 SUPPLIES

Bibles, printed seven-step instructions found after this game, two small disposable cups of water, blindfolds, paper

PREPARATION

Make two copies of the instructions included in this game.

TIP Don't provide props for teams; part of this game's fun is in finding the needed items. Kids will need access to an outdoor area so they can find dirt and sticks.

Creation Race Instructions

1. Lead a blindfolded person—representing night—to the goal line. At the goal line, have the person remove his or her blindfold to represent day and return to your starting place. Everyone shout, "Day one! It is good!"

2. Carry a cup of water to the goal line, drink it, and leave the cup at the goal line to represent earth and sky. Then run back to your team. Everyone shout, "Day two! It is good!"

3. Carry a handful of dirt to the goal line to represent the earth. Make a small hill with it and then return. Everyone shout, "Day three! It is good!"

4. Carry a small stick to the goal line. Draw a sun, moon, and star in the dirt to represent the lights. Return to your team and everyone shout, "Day four! It is good!"

5. With paper, make a bird to represent flying creatures. Carry the bird to the goal line, leave it, and return to your group. Everyone shout, "Day five! It is good!"

6. Using small sticks, make a human figure to represent humankind. Carry the stick figure to the goal line, leave it, and return to your team. Everyone shout, "Day six! It is good!"

7. All teammates run together to the goal line and sit in a circle. Everyone shout, "Day seven! Day of rest!"

ABCs of Creation

Kids brainstorm lots of things that God created.

AGES 6-9

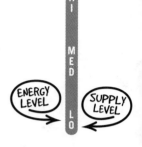

SUPPLIES

Bible, copy of the alphabet

PREPARATION

Have kids sit in a circle. Open the Bible to Genesis.

Say: **Genesis is the first book of the Bible, and it tells us about what happened when God created the earth.**

Today we'll think about things God created using the letters of the alphabet as our guide. I'll begin the game by saying, "God created the earth, and he made Adam." Then the person next to me will say, "God created the earth, and he made Adam and [something that starts with the letter B].**"**

Continue around the circle, reminding kids of their letter as necessary.

Debrief

After playing this game, ask:

- *What was hard about this game?*
- *Which thing do you think would be the hardest to create?*
- *Tell about what you think is the most amazing thing God created, and why.*

Best for
AGES 6-9

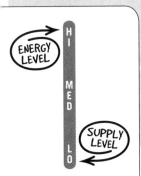
ENERGY LEVEL
HI
MED
LO
SUPPLY LEVEL

SCRIPTURE

Genesis 2:4-22

SUPPLIES

Bible

PREPARATION

Get-to-Know-You Tag

During this icebreaker, kids get to appreciate the special value of everyone in their group.

Say: **God spent time each day with Adam and Eve, and he knew all of their special qualities. Let's get to know each other. When your turn comes, say your name and describe something about yourself. Listen carefully—you may need to know this information!**

Explain that it's easier to remember someone's name if you know something about that person. Start by introducing yourself so kids have an example to follow.

Once everyone has had a turn, say: **Now we're going to play Chain Tag with a twist.** Choose someone to be "It."

Explain that as kids get tagged by It, they'll join hands with the chain of captives and help tag others.

Say: **Here's the twist: In order to keep someone you've tagged, you must say that person's name and declare his or her special quality. For example, if I'm It and I touch Samantha, I grab her hand and say very loudly, "This is Samantha and she has a pet hamster."**

If the taggers don't introduce you correctly, introduce yourself again and go free. Next time you're tagged, we'll definitely remember your name!

Debrief

After playing the game, have kids form groups of three and discuss the following.

- *What things did you learn about the kids in our group?*
- *What do you think was special about Adam and Eve?*
- *Why do you think God created you? How did God make you special?*

Say: **God creates each of us with special and unique qualities. He takes time to know us, and he appreciates our differences.**

AGES 6-9

Bustin' Loose From the Lions' Den

Kids explore courage and standing up for their beliefs.

SCRIPTURE
Daniel 6

SUPPLIES
Bible, masking tape, timer or stopwatch

PREPARATION
For every five kids, tape one big circle (10 feet across) on the floor of your room.

TIP — You'll need a big area for this game.

Read Daniel 6 aloud. Say: **You never know when you may get stuck in a den of lions. Right now, we're going to find out what kind of busting-loose-from-the-lions'-den skills we have.**

Form groups of five and have each group stand at a circle. Have each group choose one person to be "Daniel." The other four kids will be Lions. Have Daniel stand inside the circle while the Lions stand outside the circle.

Say: **Daniel will have one minute to try to flee the den without being touched by one of the Lions. To escape, Daniel must stand completely outside the circle.**

Start the timer, and have groups count how many times Daniel escapes and how many times the Lions tag him during the game. When one minute is up, have kids switch roles. Continue until all kids have had a chance to be Daniel.

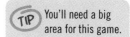
Debrief

At the end of the game, have kids summarize Daniel 6. Then ask:

- *What did you think when you learned Daniel had to go in the lion's den?*
- *What were you thinking when you first went into the lions' den?*
- *Tell about a time you felt you were surrounded by trouble or difficulty.*
- *How does God help us have courage when we're afraid?*

Say: **It's important to stand up for what we believe. God can give us the courage to always stand strong for him in every situation—even in the face of death.**

Best for

AGES 6-9

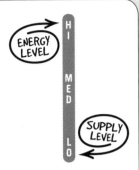

ENERGY LEVEL

HI
MED
LO

SUPPLY LEVEL

SCRIPTURE

1 Samuel 17:1-50

SUPPLIES

Bible, blindfolds, table

PREPARATION

You'll need a large playing area with a table but no chairs around it.

Stalking Goliath

Kids learn about David and Goliath.

Arrange teams of two. Kids will play this game one pair at a time. Blindfold the first pair and have them stand on either side of a table. Designate which partner is Goliath and which partner is David.

Say: **Goliath's job is to keep away from David. David's job is to catch Goliath. You can't move away from the table at any time, but you can go around, under, from side to side, or wherever. You can try to fool each other by giving false signals, too.**

Kids will have fun watching, but tell them not to give any clues as to which direction either player is going. When David catches Goliath, or after two minutes, let another pair play.

Debrief

At the end of the game, discuss the following.

- *What made this game fun?*
- *Explain how easy or difficult it was to try to catch someone when you couldn't see.*

Open your Bible and summarize what happened to David and Goliath from 1 Samuel 17:1-50. Then ask:

- *What challenges did David face in this situation?*
- *What challenges are you facing that you need God's help with?*

Say: **God is bigger than any of our problems. We can trust in God.**

AGES 6-9

Faith Followers

Kids follow a leader and learn how important it is to follow God.

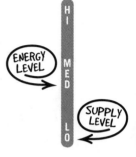

SCRIPTURE

Galatians 2:15-20

SUPPLIES

Bible, dot stickers

PREPARATION

Have kids stand in a line.

Say: **Let's see what good followers you are. In this game, one of you will be the Leader. The rest of us will be Followers and will copy the Leader's "rules." If the Leader claps his or her hands, we'll all clap our hands. Sounds easy, right? The hard part is, each time the Leader gives us a new "rule," we have to do the old "rules"—in order—first. The challenge is remembering everything the Leader tells us to do.**

Choose a willing child to be the Leader, and help the child come up with motions if needed (ideas include jumping, giving a high five to a neighbor, pinching your nose, blinking your eyes, and so on). Have the Leader stand in front of the line. The Leader can begin making motions that everyone else follows.

If a child makes a mistake, place a dot sticker on his or her shoulder and continue playing. Continue the game until everyone has at least one dot sticker.

Debrief

After you play the game, have kids sit in a circle and discuss:

- *Explain how easy or hard it was to perfectly follow the rules.*
- *Why is it hard to be perfect?*

Read aloud Galatians 2:15-20.

- *Why is it important to follow Jesus?*

Say: **The Bible tells us that following Jesus is the best thing we can do. When we follow Jesus, our actions become more like his.**

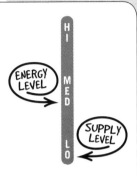

Best for

AGES 6-9

ENERGY LEVEL

SUPPLY LEVEL

SCRIPTURE

Proverbs 3:5-6

SUPPLIES

Bible, timer or stopwatch

PREPARATION

Clear the room of any obstacles. Be ready to darken the room after you've explained the game.

Lighthouse

As kids try to reach a "lighthouse," they'll learn about putting their faith in God.

Select a person to be the "Lighthouse" for the group.

Say: **In a minute, the Lighthouse will stand in one place somewhere in the dark room and whisper these words from Proverbs 3:5-6 over and over: "Trust in the Lord." You'll go out of the room and when you come back in, you will close your eyes and walk in the darkness following the voice of the Lighthouse. You have three minutes to reach the Lighthouse before time runs out, leaving you "treading water." When you've reached the Lighthouse, open your eyes, lock arms with the Lighthouse, and join in whispering, "Trust in the Lord."**

Take everyone except the Lighthouse out of the room. Have the Lighthouse take his or her place (farthest from the door works best). Turn off the lights, and let kids enter with their eyes closed. After kids are inside, give a signal to begin. After three minutes, turn on the lights to see who's left treading water, then play again.

Debrief

At the end of the game, sit in a circle, and discuss the following.

- *What was it like to use just your ears to find the Lighthouse?*
- *What is it like when you trust God?*
- *What is something you need to trust God about this week?*

AGES 6-9

Rejoice Race

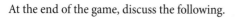

Kids think of reasons to rejoice in God.

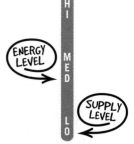

1 Thessalonians 5:16-18

Bible, chairs

Form a circle of chairs, with one less chair than the number of players.

Have all kids but one sit in the chairs. The standing child is "It" and this child will remain standing.

Say: **It may point to any seated child, and say "Rejoice in the Lord," then quickly count to 10. That person must name one thing he or she is thankful for before It reaches 10. If the child cannot think of anything that quickly, he or she becomes the new It. If It says, "Everyone rejoice in the Lord!" then everyone must quickly stand up and find a new seat while It tries to find a seat as well. The player who doesn't find a seat will become the new It.**

Play several rounds. Afterward, read aloud 1 Thessalonians 5:16-18.

Debrief

At the end of the game, discuss the following.

- *What was easy or hard about thinking of things to rejoice in God about?*
- *Why do we sometimes forget to thank God for all he does for us?*
- *What's one way you can show God you're joyful about what he's done for you?*
- *Why is it important to show thanks to God?*

Say: **We have so many reasons to thank God and express our joy. This week, take time each day to rejoice in God.**

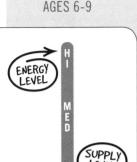

AGES 6-9

ENERGY LEVEL

HI MED LO

SUPPLY LEVEL

SCRIPTURE

Joshua 6:15-17, 20

SUPPLIES

Bible

PREPARATION

Walls Fall Down

Kids explore how to do things God's way.

Say: **Today we're going to re-enact what happened when God made the walls of Jericho fall down.**

Designate half the kids to be "Walls" and the other half to be "Israelites." Have the Walls form a circle with the Israelites outside.

Say: **When I say "Go!" the Israelites will try to get inside the Walls' circle, but only two Israelites at a time can attempt to enter. The Walls will try to keep the Israelites out. The Israelites can't run or jump at the Walls. They must get in by nudging their way through or by creating a diversion.**

Have kids form pairs. Allow kids to play, with Israelite pairs taking turns trying to get through. If some Israelites manage to get in, have the Walls reset, and give other Israelites a turn. Play for a few minutes, and then have teams switch roles.

Read aloud Joshua 6:15-17, 20. Have the Israelite group re-enact what happened in the Bible and the Wall group fall to the floor when the Israelites shout out.

Say: **If the Israelites had tried to get into Jericho on their own strength, many probably would've died in the battle. God's way may be beyond our understanding, but it's always better than our way.**

Debrief

After the game has ended, discuss the following.

- *What does this Scripture tell you about God's power?*
- *What things can be difficult to do God's way?*
- *Why does it matter that we do things God's way?*

AGES 6-9

Find Your Family

Kids learn about living in harmony with family members.

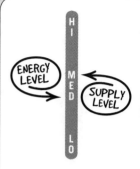

SCRIPTURE

1 Peter 3:8-9

SUPPLIES

Bible, slips of paper, pencil

PREPARATION

Beforehand, prepare sets of paper slips. Make four slips of paper for each set, and on each slip, write one family member and the same animal:

Dad _____,
Mom _____,
Sister _____,
Baby _____.

For example, you'll have a Dad Chicken, Mom Chicken, Sister Chicken, and Baby Chicken. Use a different animal for every family group. Make enough sets so everyone in your group will have a paper slip.

Form groups of four. Give each person one folded slip of paper with family member and an animal on it.

Say: **Don't look at your paper yet. When I say "Go!" walk around the room and trade papers with other people. Try to make as many exchanges as possible. Ready? Go!**

After two minutes, say: **Read your paper and find your family. You can't talk, so you'll need to find your family by acting out the animal on your paper. When you find your families, sit down on the floor in order from Dad to Mom to Sister to Baby.**

When all the "families" are together, have kids tell their real names to one another and a fun tidbit about themselves, such as their favorite ice cream or animal.

Debrief

Afterward, the family groups will discuss the following:

- *Explain what was easy or difficult about this game.*
- *What were you thinking when you found your family members?*
- *What's fun about living with a family? difficult?*

Read aloud 1 Peter 3:8-9.

- *What are ways we can live in harmony with our family members this week?*

Best for

AGES 6-9

SCRIPTURE

Ephesians 2:19-21

SUPPLIES

Bible, white paper towels, three squirt guns, three buckets of water, tape, food coloring (blue, red, and yellow)

PREPARATION

Fill three buckets of water, and add one color of food coloring to each bucket. Fill three squirt guns with the colored water before the game. Tape several white paper towels to a tree or old chair. Set the buckets five feet away from the paper towels.

TIP This game works best outside. Warn kids ahead of time to wear old clothes or have volunteers bring old T-shirts.

Little Squirt

Kids race to squirt designs on paper towels as they talk about their families.

Arrange kids into trios with each trio lined up behind a bucket. Give someone in each group a squirt gun.

Say: **Let's learn something about your families as you play this game. The first question is, "How old is the youngest person in your family?" When I say "Go!" run to the paper towels and squirt them once for every year. For example, if you have a 3-year-old brother, squirt the paper towels three times. Then run back, and give the squirt gun to the next person in your line. Ready? Go!**

Continue by having kids squirt answers to questions such as:

- *How many people are in your family?*
- *How many pets are in your family?*
- *How many cans of pop are you allowed to drink in a day?*

Every now and then, call time so you can remove the paper towels and lay them in the sun to dry. Provide fresh paper towels, and have kids continue squirting until everyone's had at least one turn. Continue asking questions so kids learn more about one another and their families.

Debrief

At the end of the game, discuss the following questions.

- *What did you learn about someone else's family?*
- *How are our families alike? different?*

Read aloud Ephesians 2:19-21; then ask:

- *What does this verse tell us about how close God is to us?*

Say: **We live with all kinds of families, and we're also God's family. He's as close to us as our own families, and we can put our faith in him.**

When the "decorated" paper towels are dry, let kids help you tape them together to form a quilt. Hang the quilt in your church or room as a reminder of each special member in God's family.

Best for

AGES 6-9

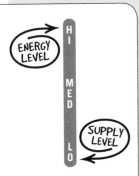

ENERGY LEVEL

SUPPLY LEVEL

HI
MED
LO

SCRIPTURE

Mark 4:35-41

SUPPLIES

Bible

PREPARATION

Stormy Seas

kids learn how God calms the storms in our lives.

Open your Bible to Mark 4:35-41, and summarize or read aloud what happened when Jesus calmed the storm.

Say: **Jesus' followers must've been scared! We're all scared sometimes, but it's great to know Jesus is always taking care of us. Let's play a game to remind us of the Bible passage.**

Form two groups, the "Followers" and the "Stormy Seas." At your signal, the Followers will pretend to row across the room to the opposite wall. To do so, the Followers will walk backward and row with their arms. The Stormy Seas will try to tag the Followers. Encourage the Stormy Seas to move their arms up and down and make wind and thunder noises.

Say: **A Stormy Sea can't tag a Follower if the Follower first says, "Be still!" If a Follower gets tagged first, though, he or she becomes a Stormy Sea and joins in the tagging.**

Play for a few minutes, and then call time. Have kids switch roles and play again.

Debrief

Let everyone sit down to rest while you discuss the following.

- *Tell about a time you were in a scary storm.*
- *Tell about other times you've been afraid.*
- *What can you do to trust God when you're afraid?*

Say: **Jesus can calm all the storms in our lives. Let's thank him for that right now!**

Close with a prayer thanking Jesus for being bigger than the fears and storms in our lives.

Fear

Angels to the Rescue

Kids play a game of Tag to learn that God sends angels to help us.

AGES 6-9

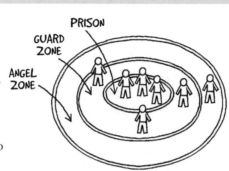
PRISON
GUARD ZONE
ANGEL ZONE

Say: **For this game, we need three teams of equal size—"Prisoners," "Guards," and "Angels."**

Help kids form the groups, and send them to their zones.

Say: **The object of this game is for the Angels to free all of the Prisoners from prison.** Point out the three zones. Say: **Angels can free Prisoners by making it through the guard zone and tagging a Prisoner in prison. If an Angel tags a Prisoner without getting caught by a Guard, the Prisoner and Angel both have safe passage back to the angel zone.**

The freed Prisoner becomes an Angel, and can begin trying to free more Prisoners.

If a Guard tags an Angel in the guard zone, that Angel becomes a Prisoner. Guards can't tag Angels in the angel zone or the prison.

Play the game three times, letting kids try each role.

Debrief

Afterward, open your Bible to Acts 12:1-19 and summarize the passage about Peter in prison. Ask:

- *What do you think it would be like to be locked in prison?*
- *Explain what you thought about Peter's response when an angel freed him from prison.*
- *What do you need God's amazing help with this week?*

Say: **God sends angels to help us and keep us safe, just as he did for Peter.**

SCRIPTURE

Acts 12:1-19

SUPPLIES

Bible, masking tape

PREPARATION

You'll need a large space with three areas marked with masking tape in large concentric circles. The inner circle is the prison, the second circle is the guard zone, and the outer circle is the angel zone.

Best for

AGES 6-9

ENERGY LEVEL

SUPPLY LEVEL

SCRIPTURE

John 8:12-14

SUPPLIES

Bible, one blindfold for each child

PREPARATION

Lightbearers

Kids search through "darkness" to find the light of Jesus and tell this good news to the others.

Invite the kids to spread out around your area.

Say: **Jesus said that until we become friends with him, it's like we're walking around in darkness. But once we find him, it's like being in the light. In this game, we'll walk around in "darkness" and then help the others find the light.**

Help kids put on blindfolds. Secretly choose one child to be the Light-bearer, silently remove his or her blindfold, and have that child stand still.

To the rest of the kids, say: **Slowly walk around the room, gently bumping into things and each other, searching for the secret Lightbearer. Whenever you find another player, whisper to each other, "How do I leave the darkness?" If both of you ask the same question, separate and keep on walking. But when someone bumps into the Lightbearer, they will hear the whispered answer, "Jesus gives the light of life." That's the signal for that player to remove his or her blindfold and become a Lightbearer, too, linking arms with the original Lightbearer. Now, whenever someone bumps into either one of them, they both whisper the Lightbearer's answer.**

As more kids find the Lightbearer and link together, the whispered message will become louder, giving a clue to those still wandering. Play until all the kids have become part of the Lightbearer group.

Debrief

At the end of the game, discuss the following.

- *What helped you find the Lightbearer?*
- *How is Jesus a light in your life?*
- *How could you work together with a friend or our church to be a lightbearer to others?*

AGES 6-9

Following Jesus

Kids learn that their actions show
others they're Jesus' followers.

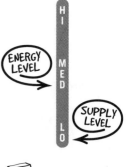

SCRIPTURE

Mark 1:14-20

SUPPLIES

Bible, timer or stopwatch

PREPARATION

Have kids stand in a circle.

Say: **The disciples didn't just follow Jesus around; they learned to care about what he cared about and to behave as Jesus behaved.**

In this game, one of you will play the part of Jesus. The rest of us will be "Disciples." If "Jesus" claps his hands, we'll all clap our hands. If Jesus pats his head, we'll all pat our heads. Sounds easy; but the hard part is, one of you will be an "Outsider" and won't know who Jesus is. You'll have to watch the group and guess which player is Jesus.

Send one child briefly outside the room. Then choose one child to be Jesus. Bring the Outsider back into the room and into the middle of the circle. Jesus will make motions that everyone else follows. Some examples of motions or actions include reaching for the sky, waving hands in the air, praying, and so on. Children stay in a circle and copy Jesus' actions. The Outsider will observe from the center of the circle and try to determine which child is playing Jesus.

After one minute, the Outsider gets three guesses about which child is Jesus. If all three guesses are incorrect, reveal Jesus' identity. After Jesus' identity is revealed, choose a new Outsider and a new Jesus. Continue playing as time permits until all children have had a turn to be either Jesus or the Outsider.

Debrief

At the end of the game, discuss the following.

- *Explain how you could tell who everyone was following.*
- *In what ways can we live and act to ensure people know we follow Jesus?*
- *What happens when we goof up and don't act in a way Jesus would?*
- *How can we remember to make choices that show we follow Jesus?*

Say: **People will know by our words and actions that we're Jesus' followers. We can make choices every day that show we follow Jesus.**

Best for

AGES 6-9

Echo Examples

Kids discover the importance of being good examples to others and choosing good examples for their own lives.

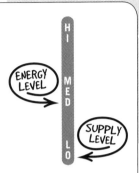

ENERGY LEVEL

SUPPLY LEVEL

SUPPLIES

PREPARATION

Form two lines and have kids stand facing each other at least 10 feet apart. The child at the end of one line will shout out a word. The other group will loudly repeat the word, and the child at the end of that line will add a second word. The first group will loudly repeat both words, and the second child in line will add a third word. The second group will then repeat all three words, and the second child in that line will add a fourth word.

Let the echo continue until one group or the other can't remember all the words and flubs the echo. Words can be Bible verses, random collections, or the world's longest run-on sentence.

Debrief

After the game, have kids sit in their groups.
Say: **In this game, each group copied the other group.**

Use the following questions for discussion.

- *What are ways people copy each other?*
- *When is copying someone a bad idea?*
- *When is it a good idea?*
- *What things about you would you want people to copy?*

Say: **The Bible tells us not to copy the ways of the world but to live for Jesus instead. As Jesus' followers, we can be an example to others. Let's ask God to help us.**

Pray, asking God to help kids be good examples of faith to the people around them.

Best for

AGES 6-9

Suit Up!

Kids learn that God is their protector.

ENERGY LEVEL — HI MED LO

SUPPLY LEVEL

SCRIPTURE

Ephesians 6:10-17

SUPPLIES

Bible, two each of the following items: caps, pairs of boots, belts, jackets

PREPARATION

Pile the two sets of clothing at one end of the room.

Gather the children and ask:

- *What are some kinds of clothing or equipment made specifically to keep you safe?*
- *What might happen if a baseball umpire forgot to put on his or her face mask and helmet?*
- *What might happen if a firefighter forgot to put on his or her coat?*

Read aloud Ephesians 6:10-17. Go to one pile of clothing, and ask a willing child to put on each piece of "armor" as you read aloud Ephesians 6:14-17 once more. When you're finished, remind the child to return the articles of clothing to the pile.

Then have children form two lines at the end of the room opposite the clothing.

Say: **Let's play a game. I'll call out a part of God's armor. The first person in each line can hop to the clothes, find and put on the article of clothing, circle twice, take it off, and hop to the back of his or her line. Then I'll call out another piece of armor.**

Continue playing until each child has had a turn.

Debrief

At the end of the game, discuss the following.

- *What was easy or hard about this game?*
- *Think of one piece of armor and describe how it can help us follow Jesus.*
- *How can you remember to "wear" God's armor every day?*

AGES 6-9

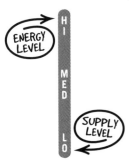

ENERGY LEVEL

SUPPLY LEVEL

SCRIPTURE

James 2:13-14

SUPPLIES

Bible

PREPARATION

Mercy Tag

Kids decide whether or not they will show mercy.

Tell kids they're going to play a game of Tag—but in this game, they can ask for mercy if someone's going to tag them. The person who's "It" can either show mercy—or not. However, if It doesn't show mercy, the tagged person has to sit out. If It decides to show mercy, the tagged person becomes It rather than having to sit out.

Choose one child to be It. Tell kids that if they want to ask for mercy, they can call out "Mercy!" when they're about to be tagged. Once everyone's been tagged, end the game or choose a new It and start over.

Debrief

Afterward, have kids discuss these questions.

- *Why did you decide you would or wouldn't show mercy?*
- *What was it like to receive—or not receive—mercy?*
- *How did people showing mercy change the game?*
- *Is there someone you can show mercy to this week?*

Read aloud James 2:13-14. Say: **Our God is a God of mercy. Even when we really don't deserve mercy, he still gives it to us. Let's remember this week to follow his example and be merciful to people around us.**

Best for

AGES 6-9

Blanket Volleyball

Kids explore how important it is to help their friends.

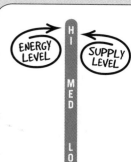

ENERGY LEVEL · HI MED LO · SUPPLY LEVEL

SCRIPTURE

1 Corinthians 3:8

SUPPLIES

Bible, rope, two chairs, small blanket (or twin sheet), several small foam rubber balls

PREPARATION

Tie a rope to two chairs and stretch it across your room.

Form two teams and have them stand on opposite sides of the rope. Give each team a small blanket or sheet. Have all team members hold the edges of their team's blanket.

Throw several small, foam rubber balls onto each team's blanket. Those team members will work together to toss the balls from their blanket over the rope to the other blanket. Encourage kids on the receiving side to try to catch all the balls. Then have them toss the balls back to the other side. Encourage the teams to work together to keep the balls in the air and off the floor.

Continue playing as time permits.

Debrief

After the game, have children gather around you. Read aloud 1 Corinthians 3:8. Ask:

- *When were you most successful at this game?*
- *Why is it important for friends to help each other?*
- *What's one way you can help a friend this week?*

Say: **Let's remember this week how important it is to love and help our friends at all times.**

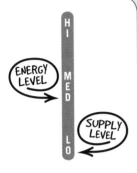

Best for

AGES 6-9

ENERGY LEVEL

SUPPLY LEVEL

HI MED LO

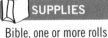

SCRIPTURE

Ecclesiastes 4:9-12

SUPPLIES

Bible, one or more rolls of crepe paper per four kids

PREPARATION

Friendship Chain

Kids discover that they can be good friends to others.

Form teams of four. Have each team stand in a separate line, then give the first person in each line a roll of crepe paper.

On "Go!" each person with the crepe paper will thread the paper around his head, across his chest, and around both legs. Then he or she will hand the paper to the next person in line who will do the same thing. This process will continue to the end of the line. If the paper breaks before all four kids are connected, the team will have to start over.

Debrief

When all the teams are done, discuss the following.

- *What was fun about this game? What was challenging?*
- *What are fun things about having friends?*
- *What's difficult about keeping friends?*

Read aloud Ecclesiastes 4:9-12. Ask:

- *How do friendships make us stronger?*
- *How does our relationship with God make our friendships even stronger?*

Best for

AGES 6-9

Do You Measure Up?

Kids realize that Jesus' love for them is too great to be measured.

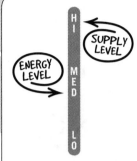

Ask kids to stand in a single-file line three feet behind the masking-tape line.

Say: **When it's your turn, you'll jump forward as far as you can with both feet.**

One at a time, let kids jump forward as far as they can. Measure how far each child jumps, and write down the distance. Don't tell kids how far they jumped—emphasize that they're not competing with each other.

When children have all had a turn to jump, add up the distances.

Say: **Wow, together you jumped a total of** [whatever the total is].

Then go on to another challenge such as jumping on one foot, jumping backward, and so on. You could also measure other distances, such as how high the children can reach or how long the line is when they hold hands and stretch out as far as they can. Each time announce only the total distance that the group attained. To help kids understand, you may want to give an example of something similar in size or length.

Debrief

Afterward, discuss the following questions.

- *What was surprising to you about how we measured our distances?*
- *What made the total measurement much bigger than it would have been if we'd just measured one person's distance?*

Read aloud John 15:9-13.

- *Describe what surprises you about Jesus' love for us.*
- *Why do you think this Scripture tells us to "remain in God's love"?*

Say: **We can measure certain things, but we can't measure Jesus' love for us because it's too big! Jesus loves us so much, he gave his life for us!**

SCRIPTURE

John 15:9-13

SUPPLIES

Bible, measuring tape, paper and pencil, masking tape

PREPARATION

Place a 2-foot masking-tape line in the middle of the floor.

Best for

AGES 6-9

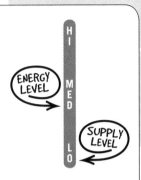
ENERGY LEVEL

SUPPLY LEVEL

SCRIPTURE

Acts 2

SUPPLIES

Bible

PREPARATION

It's Spreading

Kids make a long chain of God's love that reaches around the room.

Say: **Let's play a game to see how God's love spreads. Let's try to wrap God's love around the room.**

Determine a starting point and ask everyone to stand against the wall in a line. Have the first child run around the room and come stand with his or her foot on the starting line and hands outstretched in the direction kids will wrap around the room. As soon as the first child is in place, the second child will run and grab the hand of the first child and stand as far apart as possible while still holding hands. As soon as the second child arrives, the third child will grab the second child's hand and so on.

As kids run, have them say, "[Child's name], God loves you" to the person whose hand they grab. Keep going until kids have wrapped the room in God's love. If kids can't reach around the room, let the first child on the starting line move to the end of the line, then the second child, and so on until the kids have collectively wrapped around the room.

Debrief

Afterward, ask the following questions:

• *What did you like about spreading around the room in this game?*
• *What do you like about spreading God's love?*

Open your Bible to Acts 2 and tell them that the Bible is God's Word. Then say: **In Acts 2, we learn that when we spread God's love, our church grows! Peter talked to a crowd about God's love. More than 3,000 people came to believe in God that day! Wow! When we tell others, God's love spreads! God's love spreads around the room, our church, our homes, our neighborhoods, and the whole world!**

Stick-With-Me Tag

AGES 6-9

kids learn that God's love is so powerful that it'll never leave them.

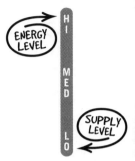

Form pairs and have partners link arms. Then choose a "Runner" and a "Chaser." The Runner and Chaser will weave in and out among the pairs. The only way a Runner can be saved from the Chaser is to link arms with one of the partners in a pair. The other partner in the pair must leave, becoming the Runner immediately. When the Runner is tagged, he or she becomes the Chaser.

Debrief

SCRIPTURE

Romans 8:35-39

SUPPLIES

Bible

PREPARATION

After the game, read aloud Romans 8:35-39.

Say: **In our game, one partner was always leaving the other. But that's not the way it is with God's love.**

Ask:

- *What does this passage tell us about God's love?*
- *What is it like to know that nothing can separate you from God's love?*
- *What does God do to show you he loves you?*

Say: **God's love is so powerful; he'll never leave us. He's always there for us, and nothing will ever, ever change that. That's great to know!**

AGES 6-9

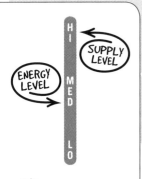

SCRIPTURE

Romans 8:38-39

SUPPLIES

Bible, an empty bulletin board, red construction paper, markers, safety scissors, straight pins or staples, two chocolate hearts per person

PREPARATION

Hide the chocolate hearts throughout the room.

ALLERGY ALERT!
See page 8

Love for Everyone

Kids see God's love for all people.

Tell kids you're all going to decorate a bulletin board. Show them how to cut out a heart from a folded square of red construction paper. Using markers, kids will write their names on their paper hearts. Then ask them to find a place on the bulletin board to attach the hearts with straight pins or staples. At the top of the bulletin board, write "Nothing can separate us from God's love" (Romans 8:38-39).

Say: **No matter what we do or where we are, God's love is with us.**

Explain that they'll now go on a treasure hunt to find God's love. Have kids look for something that might represent God's love while saying:

No matter where I happen to be,
God's love is all I see.

When someone finds a chocolate heart, that child will yell, "God's love is here!"

When everyone has found a heart, say: **Once you've found God's love, the best thing you can do is share it with others.** Have kids give their heart to someone else in the class.

Send kids on a treasure hunt again to find a second heart to give away. Ensure that each child ends up with two chocolate hearts.

Debrief

Afterward, sit in a circle to discuss the following.

- *What was your favorite part of this experience?*
- *What were you thinking when you discovered God's love?*
- *What happened when you shared your treasure with others?*
- *In what ways can we share God's love with others this week?*

Doing the Impossible

Kids attempt a tough task and learn that nothing is impossible with God.

AGES 6-9

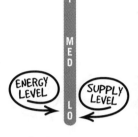

Form groups of four. Give each group an open bag of Hershey's Kisses chocolates.

Say: **Your group can eat as many Hershey's Kisses as you want—as long as you don't use your hands to unwrap them.**

Allow time for kids to attempt this task. While it's nearly impossible, applaud kids' creativity and efforts.

Debrief

Afterward, give each child a few Hershey's Kisses and discuss the following.

- *Describe what you were thinking when I gave you this challenge.*

Read aloud Matthew 19:23-26. Discuss the following questions.

- *What things are impossible for us to do that God can do?*
- *Tell about something you're facing that seems impossible.*
- *What do you think Jesus would tell you to do about that "impossible" thing?*

SCRIPTURE

Matthew 19:23-26

SUPPLIES

Bible, one bag of Hershey's Kisses chocolates per four kids

PREPARATION

ALLERGY ALERT!
See page 8

Best for

AGES 6-9

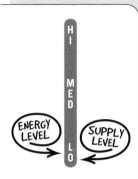

SCRIPTURE

Matthew 3:16-17

SUPPLIES

Bible

PREPARATION

Only Jesus

Kids realize that only God's Son
could do what Jesus did.

Have kids sit in a circle.

Say: **Let's play a game where we take turns sharing things we know about Jesus.**

Choose a child to start the game by turning to the person on the left and sharing one thing that only Jesus could do. For example, the child might say, "Jesus can walk on water." The child on the speaker's left will add, "Only God's Son can do that." Then that child will turn to the person on the left and repeat the first fact about Jesus and add one more. Each new speaker will repeat everything the other kids said about Jesus and add one more thing.

If a child is unable to remember one of the facts about Jesus, encourage other kids to help. Additionally, if someone can't think of something special about Jesus to add, encourage the others to help, too. Keep going until every child has added a new fact about Jesus.

Debrief

After playing this game say: **Wow! You sure remember a lot of special things about Jesus. Jesus could do things that no one else could do.**

Discuss these questions together.

- *Why do you think Jesus could do so many special things?*
- *Explain your favorite thing Jesus did and why it is your favorite.*

Read aloud Matthew 3:16-17. Say: **One day God told everyone that Jesus is his Son. Only God's Son could do all the special things that Jesus did.**

AGES 6-9

Perfect Praise

Kids balance books and discuss why
Jesus doesn't need practice.

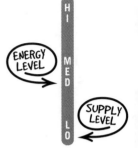

Form two teams, and have them both form their own single-file line on one side of the room. Give the first person in each line a hardcover book. Tell kids they have to balance the books on their heads with no hands, walk to the other end of the room, touch the wall, and return to the team. If they drop the book, they have to start again at the beginning. Allow time for everyone to take a turn in the relay.

SCRIPTURE

John 17:25-26

SUPPLIES

Bible, hardcover books

PREPARATION

Debrief

After the relay, ask:

- *What would have made this activity easier?*
- *Explain how important you think it is to practice when you're learning a new skill.*
- *Tell whether you think it's possible to be really good at something without practicing.*
- *What are some things you've learned to do well by practicing?*

Read aloud John 17:25-26. Say: **Practice is supposed to make perfect. But the good news is that Jesus is already perfect; he doesn't need practice to be able to do anything. When you're struggling to learn new things, take a minute to ask Jesus for help.**

Grace

AGES 6-9

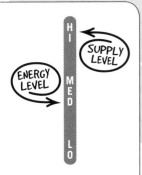

Snowball Fight

This game reminds kids of
the power of God's grace.

SCRIPTURE

Isaiah 1:18-20

SUPPLIES

Bible, newspapers,
masking tape, a timer or
stopwatch, disposable
wipes

PREPARATION

Divide your room into two
equal-sized areas with a
masking-tape line.

Form two groups. Give each group an equal amount of newspaper. On your signal, let teams make newspaper "snowballs" and quickly throw them at the opposing team for two minutes. The object is to get the most "snow" on the opponent's side before time's up.

At the end of the game, have kids collect the newspaper, and place it in your church's recycle bin. Hand out disposable wipes so kids can clean their hands.

Debrief

Gather kids together and discuss the following.

- *Describe what your hands looked and felt like after the snowball fight.*

Read aloud Isaiah 1:18-20.

- *In this game, how was the newspaper like sin?*
- *How were the wipes like God's grace?*
- *Describe whether you think God's grace ever runs out.*

Say: **God knows we're going to mess up and sin, even when we try not to. And the great news is that he'll forgive for all of our sins; his grace never runs out. Next time you're feeling grimy inside, just ask God to forgive you and he'll cleanse your heart.**

Grace

The Gift of Light

Kids try to keep their shadows from getting stepped on.

AGES 6-9

Say: **Dark places can be scary. You don't know what you might trip over or run into. But when you shine a light, the darkness is gone.**

Read aloud Ephesians 2:8-9 and say: **God gave us grace when he sent us his Son. Jesus takes away our sins.**

Give two kids flashlights, and tell them they're "light carriers." Turn on the lamp, and then dim the overhead lights. Have kids look for their shadows.

Say: **When I say "Go!" chase one another's shadows and try to step on them. If someone steps on your shadow, freeze where you are. When the light touches your shadow, you're free to move again.**

SCRIPTURE

Ephesians 2:8-9

SUPPLIES

Bible, two flashlights, lamp

PREPARATION

Place a bright lamp in one corner of the room. Test the lamp to make sure it creates clearly defined shadows when the room lights are dimmed.

Debrief

At the end of the game, discuss these questions.

- *Explain what the light did to your shadow.*
- *How are sins like or unlike the shadows before the light touched them?*
- *In what ways is Jesus like the light that touched our shadows?*

Read aloud Ephesians 2:8-9 again. Say: **It's not what you do or who you help that blesses you; it's God's grace through Jesus. All of our good-ness comes from God, and Jesus wipes away our sins.**

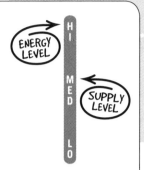

AGES 6-9

Stay Away

Kids play a version of Keep Away to help them realize that with Jesus, everyone is welcome.

SCRIPTURE

Luke 5:27-32

SUPPLIES

Bible, balloons, markers

PREPARATION

Inflate and tie off a bunch of balloons, approximately one per child (the number doesn't need to be precise).

BALLOON WARNING!
See page 8

Using markers, allow kids to draw faces on the balloons and then scatter themselves around the room. Explain that the object of the game is for kids to keep the balloons away from themselves. Encourage children to shout, "Stay away from me!" "Get away!" and "I don't want you near me!" each time they bat a balloon.

Have kids bat the balloons for a few minutes. Then call time and collect the balloons.

Debrief

Gather everyone together and discuss the following.

- *What was it like to try to keep all those balloons away from you?*
- *Are there certain people you try to keep away from in real life? Explain.*

Say: **In Jesus' day, certain people were looked down on—people like tax collectors. But those were people Jesus wanted to be with. I'll show you what I mean.**

Have a willing child read aloud Luke 5:27-32. Ask:

- *How was our balloon game like how the Pharisees and religious teachers treated tax collectors?*
- *How was our game unlike how Jesus treated tax collectors?*

Say: **In our game, we tried to keep the balloon "people" away from us. That's how the Pharisees tried to stay away from tax collectors and people like them. But Jesus came to save all people, including the people no one else wants to hang out with. That's because with Jesus, everyone is welcome!**

Best for

AGES 6-9

Bethlehem Balloons

Kids take a census of balloons as they learn about events leading up to Jesus' birth.

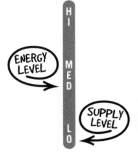

ENERGY LEVEL

SUPPLY LEVEL

SCRIPTURE

Luke 2:1-5

SUPPLIES

Bible, balloons

PREPARATION

Give each child a balloon. Ask kids to scatter around the room so they're equally spaced throughout your playing area, and have them sit.

Read aloud Luke 2:1-5.

Say: **Joseph had to take Mary to his hometown to be counted in a census.** Explain what a census is. **It's time to take a census of the balloons. We have to count all of our balloons, and to be counted they must return to their "hometowns."**

Designate the corners of your playing area as the hometowns. Assign one color to each corner.

Say: **There's one catch with the balloon census: You have to bat the balloons to the correct corners without standing up or moving.**

Tell kids to begin, and then stand back and watch the fun! When all the balloons have been batted to the corners, close the game by asking each child to go to a corner, find one balloon, and sit on it to break it. As each child breaks a balloon, help him or her count out "one," "two," and so on until kids have counted all the balloons in each corner. Collect all balloon pieces quickly and dispose of them.

Debrief

At the end of the game, discuss the following questions.

- *How easy or difficult was our census?*
- *Describe what you think it would be like to travel to a completely different city on foot for a census today.*
- *Let's count the ways we're thankful that Mary and Joseph took the tough journey to Bethlehem for the census by naming something about Jesus' birth you're grateful for.*

You'll need one balloon per child, and an equal number of balloons in four colors. Have older kids help you inflate and tie balloons before the game. (Remember that balloons are a choking hazard for young children.) Or ask an adult volunteer to help you. Place the balloons in the center of the room.

BALLOON WARNING!
See page 8

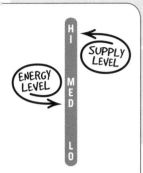

Best for

AGES 6-9

In the Dark

Kids play blindfolded to help them understand
what it's like to be blind.

SCRIPTURE

John 9:1-15, 24-34

SUPPLIES

Bible; two blindfolds;
four cups, two containing
water; paper; pencils;
towel (to clean up water
spills)

PREPARATION

Open your Bible
to John 9:1-15, 24-34,
and briefly summarize
how Jesus healed the
blind man. Count off by
twos so that the group is
divided into two equal
teams. Both teams will
send one person forward
to be blindfolded by you.

Have teammates cheer as the two blindfolded people perform these
tasks: pour water into a cup, write their names on paper, and then walk
back to the team to tag the next teammate to come forward and be
blindfolded.

Debrief

After everyone has had a turn, let kids take off their
blindfolds and discuss the following.

- *Talk about what it was like to do the tasks without being able to see.*
- *What do you think about how Jesus helped the blind man?*
- *What will you tell your friends about Jesus this week?*

AGES 6-9

Water Into Wine

Kids discover the wonder of Jesus' first miracle.

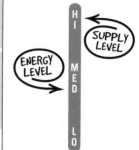

Help kids form groups of 10 or fewer and have them stand with their groups at one end of the room. If you have fewer than 10 children, keep all kids together. At the other end of the room, set up the following items so each group has its own supplies: one large pot with two packages of drink mix dumped out in the bottom, one large pot of water, one cup, and one large stirring spoon. Read aloud John 2:1-11.

Say: **You'll work as a team to change the water in this pot into "wine" in that pot.** (Point to each appropriate pot as you speak.) **Each of you will scoop out one cup of water and pour it into the other pot, then go back to your group. When everyone has poured one cup of water into the pot, each of you will take a turn stirring the pot with the spoon.** The last person in each group will scoop out a cup of "wine" from the pot to show how they turned plain water into wine.

Debrief

Afterward, discuss the following.

- *Explain whether you think Jesus had to work as hard as you all just did to change the water into wine at the wedding.*
- *Why do you think Jesus did miracles like this?*
- *What do Jesus' miracles tell us about who he is?*

Say: **We had fun changing our water into wine today, but we were pretending. Jesus really changed water into wine—it was a miracle. Jesus could do it because he's God's Son.**

SCRIPTURE

John 2:1-11

SUPPLIES

Bible; two packages of unsweetened purple drink mix for each group of 10; two large pots for each group of 10 (this will be more exciting if one of the pots for each team has a black interior so kids can't see that the color has changed); one cup for each group of 10; one large, black stirring spoon for each group of 10; and water

PREPARATION

ALLERGY ALERT!
See page 8

Best for

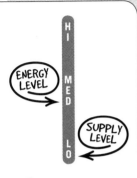

AGES 6-9

 SCRIPTURE

Mark 2:3-12

SUPPLIES

Bible, foam rubber or other soft balls (one per four children)

 **PREPARATION**

Kneezies

Kids learn how it feels to have restricted mobility and how Jesus cares for everyone's needs.

Form teams of four and have groups spread out. Direct one child on each team to put a soft ball between his or her knees. Instruct children to walk a designated distance and back again without dropping the ball. They can't use their hands to hold the ball in place. Remind children that this isn't a race, just a different way of trying to get across the room. If they drop the ball, have them pick it up and put it back between their knees and continue.

As kids do this, say: **People who have hurt their legs or are born with legs that don't work properly can't move their legs the same way that most of you do.**

When each child has had a turn, begin another relay by changing the instructions to hopping, running, or skipping with the ball between their knees.

Debrief

After playing this game, have kids discuss:

- *What was this game like for you?*
- *How could you get from place to place if you couldn't walk at all?*

Read aloud Mark 2:3-12.

- *What problems or concerns do you have that need Jesus' healing?*

Say: **It feels good to be able to run and play. The man in our passage couldn't even walk, but he had friends who cared about him so much that they took him to see Jesus. Jesus healed the man because he cared about him, too. Jesus cares about all our needs.**

AGES 6-9

Impossible? Knot!

Kids attempt a tough task and learn that nothing is impossible with God.

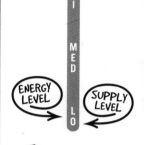

Once kids are arranged in pairs, give each pair a length of rope or string. Challenge kids to hold one end of the rope in each hand and tie a knot without letting go of the ends. One partner will attempt to tie the knot as the other partner cheers him or her on. Then let partners switch roles.

Play for several minutes. If anyone figures out the solution, have that pair sit down until the end of the game. Then they can explain the solution to the rest of the class. If no one comes up with the solution, explain it yourself: The knot can be tied by crossing your arms over your chest, so that one hand is in front of your arms and the other is behind or below them, almost like crossing your arms twice. Then lean over and pick up the ends of the rope with your arms still crossed. When you unfold your arms, a knot is automatically tied in the rope.

Matthew 28:1-10

Bible, three-foot length of string or rope for every two kids

PREPARATION

> (TIP) This game will seem impossible to kids at first, just as Jesus' resurrection must have seemed impossible at the time. But kids will realize that the game is possible, just as Jesus rising from the dead was possible because Jesus is God!

After playing the game, have partners sit down and discuss the following.

- *How impossible was this experience?*
- *How impossible is it for someone to be dead and come back to life?*
- *How do you explain Jesus coming back from the dead?*
- *How is Jesus' resurrection different from being able to tie a knot in this game?*

AGES 6-9

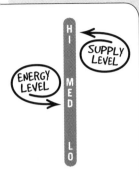

SCRIPTURE

John 20:1-18

SUPPLIES

Bible; grocery bag for each team of four kids; one scavenger-hunt list per team (the list should include the following: pebble, white napkin or piece of cloth, tissue, handful of dirt, ruler, newspaper)

PREPARATION

You'll likely need to strategically plant some of the scavenger-hunt items—one per team— prior to the game.

Plan to have one adult per team to help supervise and time the search.

Sight Seeing

Kids learn that God always keeps his word, no matter how hard it seems to believe.

Say: **Seeing can be believing. It's important to pay attention to what God puts in our paths each day, because we never know what he has in store for us. Just like Mary, we may be very surprised by what we see!**

Form teams of four. Give each team a grocery bag to take with them on their scavenger hunt. Give them approximately 10 to 15 minutes to find the items on the list and return to your room.

Shorten or lengthen the time depending on your location, availability of supplies, time constraints, and so on. You want teams to feel pressure to finish, but not be overwhelmed.

Say: **You have 10 minutes to gather the items on your team's list. That means you'll need to be back here at** [state the time kids should be back]. **If you find more than one of an item on your list, leave the extra item where you found it.**

When kids return, talk about the items they found and how these could remind them of the time Jesus appeared to Mary. Affirm everyone's ideas. If kids need help getting started, offer some of these ideas:

• The pebble could remind us of the stone that was in front of Jesus' grave.

• The napkin or cloth could remind us of the grave clothes that Jesus left behind.

• The tissue could remind us that Mary cried when she couldn't find Jesus.

• The dirt could remind us that Mary mistook Jesus for the gardener.

• The ruler could remind us that Mary called Jesus "Teacher."

• The newspaper could remind us that Mary shared the exciting news with the disciples.

• *Debrief*

Sit together and read aloud John 20:1-18. Then discuss the following.

- *Why do you think Mary mistook Jesus for the gardener?*
- *Describe a time you saw something that was hard to believe. What made you believe it was true?*
- *What's hardest for you to believe about Jesus' death and resurrection?*

Say: **Jesus' appearance to Mary reminds us that God's truth is sometimes surprising and even hard to believe—but we can always have faith in him.**

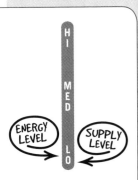

Best for

AGES 6-9

Wordly Wise

Kids are challenged to think in "heavenly" ways rather than "earthly" ways.

SCRIPTURE

Colossians 3:1-2

SUPPLIES

Bible, one foam ball or beanbag

PREPARATION

Arrange the kids in a circle around you.

Say: **In a moment, I'll say a word and toss this ball to one of you. After you catch it, I want you to say the first word that comes to your mind when you hear the word I said. Then toss the ball back to me, and I'll toss it to another person.**

Toss the ball to various children in the circle until everyone has had a turn. You could use words such as *food, sports, garden, clouds, summer, tree,* and so on.

Say: **The Bible tells us that Jesus is alive and living in heaven. Though Jesus died on the cross, he didn't die forever. Jesus was resurrected— he came back to life!**

Because Jesus is alive in heaven, let's try to think about things in heaven. Let's play our word game again, but this time, I want you to think about heavenly words.

Before you toss the ball again, give some examples of how children's responses might change. For example, when you say "song," someone might answer "angels" or "praise."

Using many of the same words as before, play the game again.

Debrief

After playing, read aloud Colossians 3:1-2. Then discuss:

- *Explain which was easier—thinking of earthly words or heavenly words.*
- *Why do you think God wants us to stay focused on heaven?*
- *How can we focus on thinking about our everyday lives in heavenly terms?*

AGES 6-9

Popping With Joy

Kids hop with joy as they learn that God gives us power to serve him.

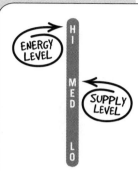

Form two teams and have team members line up single file. Put a bucket of popcorn at the center of a designated goal line and an empty bucket at the head of each team's line. Give each child a paper plate.

At your signal, have the first child on each team hop to the goal, scoop a handful of popcorn onto the paper plate, and hop back with it on the plate (not eating it—that would be a big choking hazard). Each runner will empty the popcorn into their team's bucket with the goal of spilling as little as possible. Give each team member a turn. Celebrate when both teams' buckets are full by sharing the popcorn.

Debrief

At the end of the game, read aloud Acts 3:1-9.
Say: **Imagine not being able to walk for your entire life. Then imagine being healed instantly in Jesus' name. You'd likely be hopping with joy like the man in this passage!**

Discuss the following.

- *Describe what was challenging about this game.*
- *Think of something really exciting and fun that has happened to you. What would you feel like if you couldn't tell anyone about it?*
- *What's something Jesus has done in your life that's brought you joy? How did you thank Jesus for it?*

Say: **God gives us power to serve him, and one way to serve him is to tell others about Jesus. This week, share joy with someone who needs to hear about Jesus!**

SCRIPTURE
Acts 3:1-9

SUPPLIES
Bible, popped popcorn, three clean buckets, one paper plate for each child

PREPARATION
none

ALLERGY ALERT!
See page 8

AGES 6-9

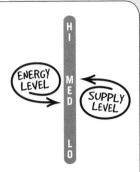

SCRIPTURE

Philippians 2:3-5

SUPPLIES

Bible, dice (one die per six children), seven chairs

PREPARATION

Place seven chairs in a straight line facing the same direction. If you have more than seven kids, make several lines of seven chairs facing the same direction.

TOPIC

Kindness

Non-Musical Chairs

Kids are encouraged to put others ahead of themselves.

Ask children to be seated in the chairs. Number the chairs from one to seven.

Roll the die, and call out the number rolled. The child who's sitting in that numbered seat must ask the person in the next-highest numbered seat to exchange seats. The person in the higher-numbered seat doesn't have to exchange, but the goal of the game is to be sitting in the lowest-numbered seat at the end of the game.

Allow three minutes of die-rolling for each round. At the end of each round, stop and recognize the child who is occupying seat number one in each group.

Debrief

After the game, read aloud Philippians 2:3-5. Ask:

- *Explain what was challenging about this game.*
- *Tell whether you put others before yourself in this game.*
- *What are some situations where you're required to put others first?*
- *What are some situations where you could choose to put others first?*

GIANT BOOK OF GAMES FOR CHILDREN'S MINISTRY

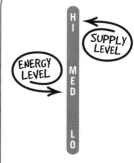

Best for

AGES 6-9

Build-Up Buddies

Kids build up one another with kind words
as they stuff a shirt with balloons.

ENERGY LEVEL

SUPPLY LEVEL

H
I
M
E
D
L
O

SCRIPTURE

1 Thessalonians 5:10-11

SUPPLIES

Bible, grocery sacks (one for each group of six), extra-large men's sweatshirts (one for each group of six), balloons (about 15 for each group of six), timer or stopwatch

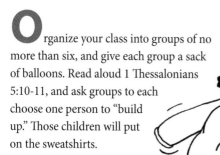

Organize your class into groups of no more than six, and give each group a sack of balloons. Read aloud 1 Thessalonians 5:10-11, and ask groups to each choose one person to "build up." Those children will put on the sweatshirts.

Ask:

• *What does it mean to "build each other up"?*

Say: **Let's pretend each balloon represents a kind word. Your group members will fill the sweatshirt with kind words by stuffing the shirt with balloons. Each time you put in a balloon, say a kind word to someone. You'll have three minutes to stuff the shirt with kind words. Ready? Go!**

After three minutes, call time and have the built-up volunteers parade around the room. Have the groups return the balloons to the sacks.

PREPARATION

Ask older kids or adult volunteers to help you inflate and tie the balloons. Put 15 balloons in each sack for each group of six.

BALLOON WARNING!
See page 8

Debrief

At the end of the game, have everyone sit and discuss the following questions.

• *What happened when you stuffed the shirts with kind words?*
• *What happens when we fill people with kind words and actions?*

Best for

AGES 6-9

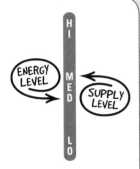

SCRIPTURE

1 John 4:7-8

SUPPLIES

Bible, handkerchief, masking tape, long rope

PREPARATION

Tie a handkerchief in the middle of a long Tug-of-War rope.

Love Tug

In this Tug-of-War game, kids learn about sharing Jesus' love with others.

Gather evenly-matched teams for pulling. Mark off two lines about three feet apart in the middle of your play area with masking tape. Position the rope so that the handkerchief hangs in between the two maskin-tape lines.

Say: **Pretend this handkerchief is someone who doesn't know Jesus. He feels like his life is pulled in many directions.**

Have kids try to pull the handkerchief over to their team's side. When one team has accomplished the goal, have them huddle to consider what they might say to the "handkerchief person" to share their faith in Jesus. Play the game several times, making sure both teams have an opportunity to share.

Debrief

At the end of the game, read aloud 1 John 4:7-8. Then discuss the following.

- *How do people get pulled in different directions?*
- *How can you help those people know and follow Jesus?*
- *How can you be good examples of who Jesus is?*

Loving Others

Welcome to the Neighborhood

AGES 6-9

Kids discover what it means to love other people more than themselves.

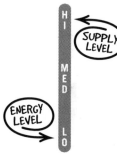

Say: **We're going to learn about God's definition of a neighbor.**

As a group, discuss the following.

- *Tell about your neighbors.*
- *Tell me a few things about one of your neighbors.*

Allow several kids to give you information about people who live near them—people they consider their neighbors.

Have kids wash their hands before beginning. Then give each child a plate with four full graham crackers on it. Small groups can share a bowl of frosting or cream cheese. However, allow each child to have his or her own plastic knife. Place the decorating items in the middle of the tables.

Explain that kids will each make a house to eat later. They'll use frosting or cream cheese as "mortar" to hold the crackers together, and then decorate the house with their favorite snack items. Make sure children aren't licking their hands or knives during this process! Give kids five to 10 minutes to complete their house.

When decorating time has passed, have kids sit around the table.

Turn on the praise music and say: **Now, we'll pass our houses to the left. When I stop the music, stop passing. I'll restart the music, and you'll pass the houses to the right. Pass the houses until I stop the music completely and tell you to eat.**

After children have traded their houses, some perhaps more than once, each child gets to eat the graham-cracker house that is sitting in front of him or her.

SCRIPTURE
Luke 10:25-37

SUPPLIES
Bible; tables; chairs; praise music and a music player; four full graham crackers per child; frosting or cream cheese; one small bowl per group; plastic knives; paper plates; edible decorations (pretzels, licorice, jelly beans, M&M's candies, and so on)

PREPARATION
Post allergy information for parents ahead of time, noting what food items will be present.

ALLERGY ALERT!
See page 8

Debrief

As children eat their snacks, summarize Luke 10:25-37.

Say: **Today you shared your food with a person who may or may not live near you. That person is still your neighbor.**

Just as we traded our food today, and perhaps gave up a snack that we really wanted, the good Samaritan gave up some of his time and money to take care of someone he didn't even know. The good Samaritan understood that God wants us to love everyone as our neighbor.

Have kids discuss these questions.

- *What about this game was easy or difficult for you?*
- *Based on the passage and our game today, how would you define a neighbor?*
- *What's one thing you can do this week to fulfill Jesus' command to "love your neighbor as yourself"?*

AGES 6-9

Honor Tag

Kids discover that it's fun to encourage others with kind words.

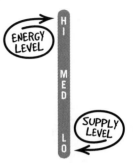

Hebrews 10:23-25

Bible

Say: **We're going to play a game called Honor Tag. In this game, the only way we can move around is by shuffling backward. Both feet have to stay in contact with the floor at all times. I'll be "It" first. When I tag someone, I'll yell "Honor Tag!" and everyone has to freeze. Then I'll honor and say nice things about the person I tagged. That person becomes It, and I sit down.**

When everyone understands, say: **Let's play!**

Keep playing until everyone has tagged and honored someone and everyone is seated. You may want to stand again at the end of the game so that the final child can tag you and honor you and sit down. That way everyone will have a full turn.

Debrief

After the game, have kids sit in a circle. Read aloud Hebrews 10:23-25. Discuss the following.

- *Why is it good to say kind things about each other?*
- *How can we remember to say kind things to each other?*
- *Tell about one thing you'll do this week to show kindness to someone.*

Best for

AGES 6-9

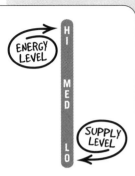

 SCRIPTURE

John 4:1-10

 SUPPLIES

Bible

 PREPARATION

Runaway Tag

Kids play a "runaway" game and talk about how Jesus embraced people that others stay away from.

Assign each child a number. Explain that you're going to play Tag. When you call out a number, the person with that number is "It" and will chase the others. Anyone who gets tagged freezes in place. But every minute or so, you'll call out a new number. When you call out a new number, everyone who's frozen is free and the person who has the number you called becomes the new It.

Play for several minutes, calling out new numbers randomly and as often as you like. Then have children sit down.

Debrief

Discuss the following.

- *What was this game like for you?*
- *Why do you think we avoid some people in real life?*

Read aloud John 4:1-10 Say: **Jesus loves everyone, no matter what.**

Ask children to discuss the following.

- *Without saying any names, tell about a person who people run away from.*
- *What can you do this week to let that person know Jesus won't run away from him or her and neither will you?*

Beach Ball Madness

Kids discover that life is easier with the Ten Commandments.

AGES 6-9

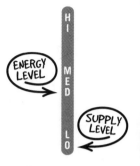

In groups of no more than six, ask children to form circles.

Say: **Okay, I think everyone is ready to play the game. Ready, go!**

After saying "Go!" toss a ball into each circle without any further instructions. Let the kids bounce the ball around and grumble for a few moments about not knowing what to do.

Then give children the actual instructions for the game.

Say: **It seems like no one knows how to play this game. The person who's holding the ball right now must make an easy toss to another person in the circle. That person then makes a toss to a different person in the circle. Do that until each person has had a turn to catch and toss the ball. The order in which you tossed the ball is the pattern you must follow. Continue to toss the ball in that order.**

Once kids have their patterns established, let them repeat the pattern several times. You can make the game more challenging by having each group toss two balls around the pattern.

SCRIPTURE

Exodus 20:1-17

SUPPLIES

Bible, one beach ball or kick ball for every six kids

PREPARATION

Debrief

After the game, read aloud Exodus 20:1-17 and discuss the following.

- *What was it like when I told you to start a game without any instructions?*
- *Why do rules make games fun?*
- *What would happen if there were no rules in games?*
- *How are the Ten Commandments like rules in a game?*
- *How do the Ten Commandments make it easier to live with other people?*

Say: **The Ten Commandments are rules that help us make better choices in life. Playing by God's rules helps us all.**

Best for

AGES 6-9

ENERGY LEVEL

HI
MED
LO

SUPPLY LEVEL

Single-Minded

Kids learn to stand up to negative influences and resist peer pressure.

 SCRIPTURE

James 1:5-8 (NIV)

 SUPPLIES

Bible, string or yarn, scissors

 **PREPARATION**

Say: **Today we'll discover how we have the choice to stand up for what's right, even when friends try to get us to do what's wrong. When friends try to get us to do something we don't want to do, that's called peer pressure.**

Form pairs. If you have an uneven number, form one group of three. Using string, tie partners together side by side. Tell children they can't talk during this game.

Call out the following commands and give children time to follow.

- **Run to the side.**
- **Hop up and down.**
- **Lie on your side.**
- **Go around in a circle.**

Debrief

Afterward, read aloud James 1:5-8 (NIV). Then discuss the following.

- *Explain how difficult it was to work together.*
- *What do you think it means to be double-minded?*
- *How was this game like being double-minded?*
- *Explain whether you think a double-minded person is more or less likely to give in to peer pressure.*
- *According to James, how can we be single-minded?*

Say: **Having two brains working together is like being double-minded. There are two minds thinking two different things. Let's play the game again where you can talk and see what it's like to be single-minded.**

Play the game again and allow kids to talk. Then ask:

- *How was the game different this time?*
- *How can talking to God help us be single-minded?*

GIANT BOOK OF GAMES FOR CHILDREN'S MINISTRY

AGES 6-9

Not Easily Broken

Kids experiment to see how standing firm together makes them stronger.

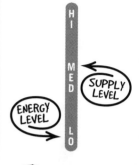

SCRIPTURE

Ecclesiastes 4:9-12

SUPPLIES

Bible, craft sticks, pencils

PREPARATION

Give each child a craft stick and a pencil to use to write their names on their sticks. Then ask kids to think of one thing that makes life tough for them. This might be schoolwork, kids who make fun of them, problems at home, worries, and so on.

Say: **Your stick will represent you. As you think of your problem, break your stick in half.** Ask:

• *Was it easy or hard to break the stick?*

Open your Bible and read aloud Ecclesiastes 4:9-12.

Give children a few more craft sticks each to write their names on, and then have them form groups of five to seven. One child in each group will share the problem he or she was thinking of earlier. Then each child in the group will give his or her craft stick to the child who shared and say, "I'll stand with you." The child who shared will put all the craft sticks into one stack and try to break them. Most children won't be able to break this many sticks at once.

Debrief

Afterward, discuss the following.

• *Why was it more difficult to break the sticks?*
• *How would having friends and family members standing with you help you stand firm against your specific problem?*
• *Tell about a person you stand with against a problem.*

Say: **Just as the sticks were hard to break when they were together, we can stand firm with others so nothing can move us or break us away from our faith. God has given us each other so no one has to stand alone. We can stand firm together.**

Upper Elementary GAMES

Preteens are ready for a challenge—and these games deliver! Not only will these games get them thinking—they'll get them cheering! These games promote cooperation, relationship-building, and deeper learning through thoughtful experiences and discussion.

Kids between the ages of 10 and 12 love games that stretch them physically and mentally. They're yearning to deepen their friendships and are beginning to grapple with all kinds of questions. The games in this section bring all the things they're craving—with an added helping of super-awesome fun!

Dig in!

AGES 10-12

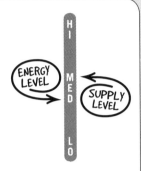

ENERGY LEVEL

SUPPLY LEVEL

SCRIPTURE

Genesis 12:1-4

SUPPLIES

Bible; two or more identical sets of toys materials (such as Lincoln Logs, Tinkertoys, or LEGOS building blocks); copies of a pictured structure that kids can build—but without the written instructions from the toy leaflet, and copies of both the picture and the written instructions from the toy leaflet

PREPARATION

Make copies of the toy leaflet instructions and pictures of the structure(s) according to instructions in the supply list above.

Build It With Blueprints

Kids work together to build something fun as they learn the value of having directions.

Based on the size of your group and the number of building sets you have available, have kids form an even number of groups. Hold up one of the building sets and say: **We're going to work together in groups to build this.**

Show the picture and name the structure they're building. Explain that you're adding a twist to this project.

Say: **God told Abram to leave his home and travel to a new land. Along the way, God gave Abram simple—but important—instructions to guide him on the journey. I'm going to give half of you a picture of the** [name the structure]. **The rest will have a picture plus instructions.**

Encourage groups to have fun building the toy or inventing the steps themselves while looking at the picture.

Debrief

When everyone finishes their structures, discuss the following.

- *What was difficult about building the structure without directions and only a picture?*
- *In what ways did the instructions help those who had them?*

Read aloud Genesis 12:1-4 and then ask:

- *What do you think of the directions Abram got from God?*
- *How might Abram's life have been different if he'd had no instructions?*
- *What do you think of the directions God has given you for your life?*

Say: **God always gives us helpful direction when he asks us to do something; it's up to us to go where God directs us.**

Best for

AGES 10-12

Absolute Truth

Kids share true statements and learn
that the Bible is absolutely true.

SCRIPTURE

Psalm 119:159-160

SUPPLIES

Bible, foam ball or
beanbag, music and a
music player

PREPARATION

Gather kids together to hold hands and form a circle facing each other.

Say: **Sometimes when people tell us things, we wonder if what we hear is the truth. In this game, we won't have to wonder because everyone must tell the truth while playing it. That's a rule!**

I'll play some music and introduce a small item into the circle that you'll toss back and forth as the music plays. When the music stops, whoever has the item will step into the center of the circle and share one true personal thing. For example, you might say, "I'm the youngest person in my family," or "Pizza is my favorite food."

Play until everyone has had a turn in the middle or time runs out.

Debrief

Afterward, say: **In this game you all shared true things. There wasn't any reason to wonder if people were being honest—that was the rule for our game.**

Sit together and discuss the following.

- *What did you learn about people that you didn't already know?*
- *How easy or difficult was it to come up with something true to share? Why?*

Read aloud Psalm 119:159-160. Say: **The Bible tells us that all of God's words are true.**

Ask:

- *How can this verse help us remember to trust God and his Word, the Bible?*

Say: **The Bible is true. We can trust everything it says.**

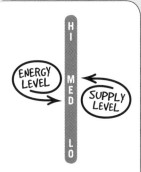

AGES 10-12

Apples and Oranges

This crazy game lets kids discover that everyone is important in God's family.

SCRIPTURE

1 Corinthians 12:14-21

SUPPLIES

Bible, an apple, an orange, one individual pack of fruit snacks per child

PREPARATION

ALLERGY ALERT!
See page 8

Arrange the entire group into a circle.

Say: **The key to this game is that you can't pass the fruit with your hands. You can use your feet, elbows, or knees to pass the fruit. One of you will pass an apple to the right around the circle. Another will pass an orange to the left around the circle. If someone drops the fruit, or it touches the ground, that player must close his or her eyes to continue playing.**

Play until only one person's eyes remain open, then collect the fruit.

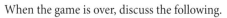
Debrief

When the game is over, discuss the following.

- *What was easy or difficult about this game, and why?*
- *How did playing with your eyes closed affect the game?*

Read aloud 1 Corinthians 12:14-21. Ask:

- *What do you think this Scripture means?*
- *How is what this Scripture says like or unlike what happened in our game?*

Brainstorm some contributions that people can make to the body of Christ. Then celebrate everyone's special role in God's family by enjoying fruit snacks together.

Body of Christ

AGES 10-12

Avalanche

Kids work together to complete a challenge while they learn the importance of each person.

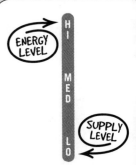

Place each player into a group of four or five kids. Give each group a sheet of construction paper. On "Go!" each team will try to get all of its team members to stand on its sheet of paper and stay there together for five seconds. (Don't let anyone give up!)

Debrief

Afterward, ask:

- *What did you have to do to stop the avalanche of falling people?*
- *How are those things like or unlike the things we have to do to be the kind of church God wants us to be?*
- *Explain what happens to our church if someone refuses to do one of these things? Give examples if kids need help.*

Read aloud Romans 15:1-7. Then close in prayer, asking God to help your group live out the verses in this passage.

SCRIPTURE

Romans 15:1-7

SUPPLIES

Bible, one sheet of construction paper per four or five kids

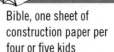

PREPARATION

Best for

AGES 10-12

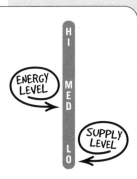

ENERGY
LEVEL

SUPPLY
LEVEL

SCRIPTURE

Luke 10:25-28

SUPPLIES

Bible, paper and pens

PREPARATION

Off Balance

Through a physical challenge, kids discover the importance of maintaining priorities.

Form groups of four. Have one person from each group try to balance on one foot as the other people in the group help the person for 30 seconds. Then call time and have the group try to hinder the person from balancing on one foot by gently pushing on the person with one finger. After 30 seconds, switch roles so another child gets to try balancing. Play until each person has had a turn balancing.

Debrief

Afterward, gather everyone together to talk about the following.

- *Describe what it was like to try to balance with help. with resistance.*
- *How did others help you balance?*
- *What was it like to be pushed off balance when you were trying to stay up?*

Say: **"Balance" is a word people use to describe when people live by their priorities—by what's important. And when someone's life is balanced, they aren't overdoing things in one area and neglecting other areas.**

Ask:

- *What are ways people lose balance in their lives?*
- *When have you been out of balance in your life?*
- *How is this experience similar to what happens when you lose balance in life?*

Say: **The best way to stay balanced is to live by your priorities. Listen to this passage that tells us what our first two priorities should be.**

Read aloud Luke 10:25-28. Have kids form pairs and list their top-10 priorities. Then have partners discuss how they can stay balanced with those priorities. Discuss God's top two priorities and how they fit in the kids' lives.

AGES 10-12

It's in the Bag

Kids discover that the Bible is useful
for making good decisions.

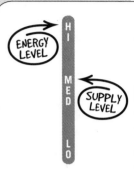

SCRIPTURE

Hebrews 4:12-13 (NIV)

SUPPLIES

Bible; masking tape; two trash bags; two sets of seven pictures of living or active things, with one of the pictures in each set being a Bible

PREPARATION

Create two parallel masking tape lines on the floor, about five feet apart.

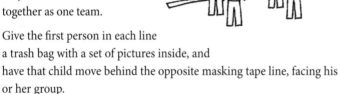

Coordinate the formation of two groups. Ask each group to line up single file behind one of the masking tape lines, facing the other line. If your group is very small, have them all work together as one team.

Give the first person in each line a trash bag with a set of pictures inside, and have that child move behind the opposite masking tape line, facing his or her group.

Say: **Your job is to think of "living and active" things. When your teammate throws the bag to you, catch it, then call out something living and active that no one else has named. Don't open the bag yet, just toss it back to your teammate, and run across to stand behind him or her. Let's see how long it takes you to get all your team members across.** Continue until everyone has gone back and forth.

Play several rounds. It gets more difficult to come up with new items the longer you play.

When groups have finished, ask someone in each group to open their team's bag.

Say: **Inside each bag are pictures of things that are living and active. Tell everyone what you have in your bag.**

Give teams a chance to show their pictures.

It's in the Bag

continued

After playing this game, discuss:

- *Why do you think a picture of the Bible was in your bag as a living and active thing?*

Read aloud Hebrews 4:12-13 (NIV).

Ask kids to think about the following.

- *How is the Bible "living and active"?*
- *What difference can the Bible make in our lives?*

Say: **The Bible is living and active, and that means that it can help us today. When we have decisions to make, the Bible can help us know the right thing to do.**

Debrief

AGES 10-12

Packing-Peanut Pass

Kids learn why not to get stuck in bad habits.

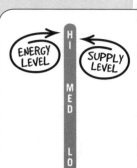

With kids separated into two lines, hand out a pair of non-latex gloves for each child to wear. Place a large bowl of packing peanuts at one end of each line and a large empty bowl at the other end. Spray everyone's gloves with aerosol adhesive being careful that kids don't inhale it.

SCRIPTURE

Psalm 25:8-10

SUPPLIES

Bible, a pair of non-latex gloves for each child, four large bowls, foam packing peanuts, aerosol spray adhesive, trash bags, tarp

Say: **When I say "Pass the peanuts," the first person will grab peanuts from the bowl and begin passing peanuts down the line. The last person in each row will put the packing peanuts in the empty bowl. Ready? Pass the peanuts!**

PREPARATION

Place the packing peanuts in two bowls. Set out a tarp, or play outside.

Play the game and listen to the laughter! Keep trash bags nearby for easy cleanup.

Debrief

At the end of the game, discuss the following questions.

- *What was this game like for you?*
- *Why was it so difficult to get peanuts unstuck from your hands?*
- *How are sticky gloves like getting stuck in bad habits?*

Read aloud Psalm 25:8-10.

Ask:

- *How can God help us choose to avoid bad habits?*

Say: **Just as it was hard to keep the packing peanuts from sticking to your hands, it can be hard to stop bad habits. But God always helps us make the right choices!**

AGES 10-12

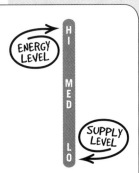

SUPPLIES

Bible, assorted small stickers

PREPARATION

Sticker Friends

Kids "sticker" others to get them to be part of their group.

Divide the group into two cliques, and allow each clique to invent a name for themselves. Place a sticker on the back of each person in the first clique. Out of sight of the other clique, give a few people in the first clique extra stickers, which they can conceal in their hands. The other kids in this clique will pretend to have stickers in their hands. Tell the second clique, who won't have any stickers at all, that they must try to keep the first clique from sticking stickers on their backs.

Begin the game, allowing the first clique to chase the second clique and either pretend to put stickers on their backs or actually do so.

When the first clique has given away all its extra stickers, stop the game. Players who now have stickers become part of the first clique.

Hand out more stickers as needed and repeat the game until everyone's been "stickered" into one clique which is now a group instead. Invite kids to come up with a creative name for the combined group.

Debrief

At the end of the game, discuss these questions.

- *What was it like to "sticker" other people into your clique?*
- *What was it like to be brought into a new clique?*
- *What are cliques like at your school?*
- *Why do you think it's important to welcome new friends into our lives?*

Say: **Choose your friends wisely, not because of which clique they belong to. And remember, your most important friendship is with Jesus. Be a good friend to others, to yourself, and to Jesus—and you won't go wrong!**

AGES 10-12

Keep It Together

As kids work in teams, they'll explore
the concept of belonging.

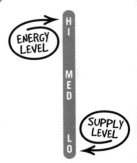

ENERGY LEVEL

SUPPLY LEVEL

Invite everyone to form a large circle. Ask for two willing kids to be in the middle.

Say: **Those of you in the circle, try to pass the ball without letting the kids in the middle get it. Kids in the middle, you work together to intercept the ball. If you're successful, or if you cause the ball to go outside the circle, then the person who threw the ball will join you in the middle.**

Play until all or almost all of the kids are in the middle. Repeat the game as long as kids show interest.

Debrief

Afterward, read aloud 1 Corinthians 1:10-12.
Then discuss:

- *What do you think living in harmony with each other means, according to this Scripture?*
- *What was it like to be on the outside of the circle? the inside?*
- *How was this experience similar to or different from being on the inside or outside of a group of people?*
- *What are ways we can ensure people always feel as if they're part of the group?*

SCRIPTURE

1 Corinthians 1:10-12

SUPPLIES

Bible, ball

PREPARATION

Best for

AGES 10-12

SCRIPTURE

Luke 1:13-20

SUPPLIES

Bible; four straws, one baseball-sized lump of clay, three wiggle eyes, five 6-inch lengths of yarn, and a metal washer per four kids (plus one extra set)

PREPARATION

For each team of four, make a kit that includes four straws, one lump of clay, three wiggle eyes, five 6-inch yarn strips, and a metal washer. Make an extra kit for yourself. Using your kit, build a creature or contraption with all of the supplies. Then hide your creature outside your room.

Loose Lips

This game challenges kids to trust and communicate God's Word.

Form teams of four, and have each team choose one person to be their director. Take all the directors out to view your model. Allow two minutes for them to memorize the object.

When directors return to their teams, say: **For this task, the directors aren't allowed to speak. They can only use gestures to give directions to their teammates. Each team has five minutes to try to build an exact replica of the model your director just viewed. Ready? Go!**

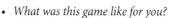

Debrief

When time's up, show teams your model. Ask:

- *What was this game like for you?*
- *What was challenging about your director not being able to talk?*
- *How did your team try to understand your director without words?*

Read aloud Luke 1:13-20. Then ask:

- *When we doubt God's Word, what does that do to our ability to communicate it?*

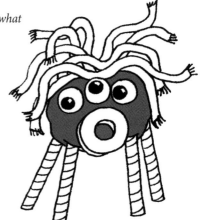

AGES 10-12

Switcheroo!

Kids learn about spreading the good news by communicating with one another.

SCRIPTURE

1 Corinthians 15:3-4

SUPPLIES

Bible, masking tape

PREPARATION

Place two long strips of masking tape parallel to each other about eight inches apart and long enough so all of the kids can stand with one foot on each line.

Have kids find a place on the tape lines with one foot on each line and all facing the same direction.

Say: **Now pull a "switcheroo" by lining up according to birthdays— kids with January birthdays at one end and December birthdays at the other end. As you move, you'll always have to have a foot on at least one line.**

Allow time for kids to rearrange.

Then say: **Now pull another switcheroo by reversing your positions. That is, the January and December birthdays must switch places, and kids in between must arrange themselves in sequence again. You'll need to communicate and help one another move along the line.**

Continue as long as time allows using different ways for kids to organize themselves. For example, you might arrange kids alphabetically, based on height, or by what kind of pet they have or want.

Debrief

At the end of the game, discuss the following questions.

- *Why was it important to communicate during this game?*
- *What happened when you didn't communicate well?*

Read aloud 1 Corinthians 15:3-4. Then ask:

- *Why does communicating the good news about Jesus matter?*
- *In what ways can we communicate what we know about Jesus to others?*

Say: **We can tell everyone that Jesus saves us from our sins. Good news!**

Best for

AGES 10-12

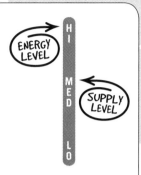

ENERGY LEVEL

SUPPLY LEVEL

H I

M E D

L O

SCRIPTURE

Genesis 1:6-7

SUPPLIES

Bible; two buckets full of water; two large, empty buckets; two large sponges

PREPARATION

Fill the buckets with water. This game would be best to play outside.

Water Split

Kids enjoy a wet-and-wild challenge perfect for summer.

Read aloud Genesis 1:6-7. Say: **We're going to experience a little bit of what it was like when God separated the waters of heaven and earth when he created the world.**

Divide the group into two teams. Have teams line up with a full bucket of water in front of each line and an empty bucket behind each line. On "Go!" the first person in each line will soak a sponge in the bucket of water. One by one, kids will pass the sponge over their heads to the end of the line.

The last person in line will squeeze out the sponge into the empty bucket, and then kids will pass the sponge back up the line to repeat. The goal is for both teams to fill their empty buckets.

Debrief

At the end of the game, discuss the following.

- *What was the most challenging part of this game?*

Read aloud Genesis 1:6-7 again. Ask:

- *Why do you think God made the world the way he did?*
- *What is your favorite thing that God created? Explain why.*

Close in prayer, thanking God for making the world for us to live in.

AGES 10-12

No-Hands Wrestling

Kids realize that we're all helpless without God.

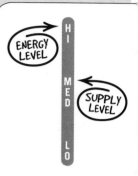

Ask two willing kids who are close to the same size to begin the game. Have each of these two players step inside a sleeping bag, then kneel inside the circle. Secure the drawstring and zipper of each sleeping bag above the shoulders of each player with their arms inside the bag.

Say: **The object of the game is for one player to make the other player cross the tape line and go outside the circle. Players can gently push, pull, or wrestle, but they must stay inside their sleeping bags and remain kneeling. Let's cheer on our no-hands wrestlers!**

Limit each match to about one minute. If any part of a player's body or sleeping bag crosses the line, that pair is finished and two new players take a turn. Ensure opponents are always about the same size and weight. If you have mostly younger kids, make the circle smaller. Let everyone have a turn at no-hands wrestling, and keep close watch so no one gets rough.

SCRIPTURE

Exodus 14:13-14

SUPPLIES

Bible, two sleeping bags with drawstring tops, masking tape

PREPARATION

This game is best played on a carpeted surface. Use masking tape to create a circle on the floor about six feet in diameter. Clear the area of any obstacles.

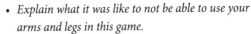

After the game, discuss the following.

- *Explain what it was like to not be able to use your arms and legs in this game.*
- *How was this experience like trying to handle your problems on your own, without God?*

Read aloud Exodus 14:13-14.

- *Angry Egyptian soldiers were chasing Moses' people. Knowing that, what about this Scripture surprises you?*
- *Why do you think God wants to help us solve our problems?*
- *How can we remember to rely on God when problems come?*

Encourage kids to turn to God with their problems. Say: **We don't have the tools, information, or power to fight all our battles...but God does!**

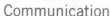

Best for
AGES 10-12

Gossip Potato Pass

Kids learn why gossip is tough on friendships.

ENERGY LEVEL — HI MED LO — SUPPLY LEVEL

Begin by arranging kids in two lines. Give the first child in each line a potato.

Say: **On "Go!" each team must pass the potato—behind your backs. Before anyone can pass the potato, he or she must silently read the message on it and then pass the potato along the line. All team members have to get the message exactly right, so do your best to remember it well!**

Signal to begin. In the first round, give teams only 15 seconds to complete the game, no matter how far the potatoes get. Have kids from both teams state the message as they remember it. Play again, giving more time. Continue several rounds with extended time, until both teams get the message right. At the end of the game, collect the potatoes.

- *Debrief* - - -

At the end of the game, read aloud Proverbs 16:27-28. Then discuss the following.

- *Explain whether getting the message right was difficult or easy.*
- *Tell about a time someone passed on a wrong message about you or a friend.*
- *What is it like to be gossiped about?*
- *What does this verse tell us about gossip? about friends?*

Say: **It's easy to misunderstand someone's situation and tell others incorrectly about it. That's why gossip is so tough on close friendships.**

SCRIPTURE

Proverbs 16:27-28

SUPPLIES

Bible, two potatoes, paper, marker, clear packing tape

PREPARATION

On the paper, write the following sentence in this broken manner, which is more difficult to read: "LU CYLO VESJES USA ND JE SUSL OVE SLUCY" ("LUCY LOVES JESUS AND JESUS LOVES LUCY"). Tape your message to each potato, and place potatoes with the message side down so kids can't read it before the game starts.

ALLERGY ALERT!
See page 8

AGES 10-12

Hard Heart or Soft Heart?

kids race to soften frozen bubble gum and explore the condition of their hearts.

SCRIPTURE

1 John 3:11-12

SUPPLIES

Bible, one piece of bubble gum per child

PREPARATION

About 24 hours before the game, freeze individual pieces of bubble gum.

ALLERGY ALERT!
See page 8

Read aloud 1 John 3:11-12, and then say: **Let's play a game to show what a cold, hateful heart like Cain's might feel like.**

Give each child a frozen piece of bubble gum. As kids try to soften it in their mouths, say: **When your "cold heart" gets warm enough, race to blow the first bubble.**

Remind kids not to bite down hard on their frozen gum. If the gum is extremely hard, let it thaw a little before beginning to prevent accidental tooth breakage.

Debrief

After all the kids have blown bubbles, ask:

- *What did you have to do to successfully blow a bubble?*
- *How was your cold gum like a cold heart?*
- *What things might be difficult to do if your heart is cold?*
- *What do we have to do to keep our hearts from becoming cold and hateful?*

Best for

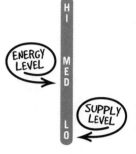

AGES 10-12

In Knots

Kids learn about working through a tangled conflict.

SCRIPTURE

Colossians 3:13-14

SUPPLIES

Bible

PREPARATION

Bring the whole group of kids together in a tight circle and have them stretch their arms toward the center. Each child will grab a different person's hand with each of his or her hands.

Say: **We have quite a knot here. Let's work together to untie it. But whatever you do, don't let go of the hands you're holding on to right now.**

Have kids go under or over each other's arms to work out the human knot. You may need to help direct the process.

Debrief

After everyone is untangled, discuss the following.

- *Explain what the toughest part of this game was, and why.*
- *How does this experience remind you of some of the "knots" of conflict you have to untangle in life each day?*

Read aloud Colossians 3:13-14. Then ask:

- *What instructions does God give us for untangling conflicts with others?*
- *How can you use this passage to undo—or avoid—knots in your relationships?*

AGES 10-12

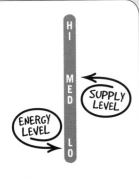

SCRIPTURE

Matthew 5:8-9

SUPPLIES

Bible, white paper, blue
and yellow crayons

PREPARATION

Color My World

Kids learn about resolving conflicts peacefully.

Ask kids to form pairs. Give each pair one sheet of plain white paper to share, and give one partner a blue crayon and the other a yellow crayon.

Say: **When I say "Go!" each of you will race against your partner to color as much of the paper as possible. You will both be coloring at the same time to see who colors more of the page.** Allow time.

When the papers are completely colored, tell partners to trade crayons.

Say: **Now your task is to work together to make your paper completely green as fast as you can by coloring over your first color with your new color.** Allow time.

Debrief

Afterward, discuss the following.

- *Explain what you were thinking or feeling during the first part of this task.*
- *What is different about competing with someone and cooperating with that person?*

Read aloud Matthew 5:8-9. Then ask:

- *What made the second part of this task a more peaceful experience?*
- *How can you be a peacemaker at school? at home?*

AGES 10-12

We Can Do It!

In this icebreaker, kids see the importance of teamwork in the body of Christ.

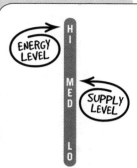

SCRIPTURE

1 Corinthians 14:10-12

SUPPLIES

Bible, index cards, pencil, clear tape or masking tape

PREPARATION

Set aside a stack of blank index cards. On the rest of the cards, write a skill or talent that one or more of your kids might have, at least one card per child (it's okay to repeat skills). Place the tape and pencil at one end of the room.

Say: **Today we're going to play a game that helps us get to know each other better and celebrates things we can do.**

Start by introducing yourself and naming one activity you enjoy. Encourage each child to do the same, also naming a favorite activity. Some kids might be modest or shy about naming their favorite activities, so be prepared with some suggestions. ("What games do you like to play with friends?" "What is your favorite book or movie?")

Ask everyone to line up against one wall in your room.

Say: **It was fun to meet each other and discover activities we enjoy. Now I'm going to read some things that we might be good at. If what I read is true for you, run by, grab the card from me, and run to the other end of the room. As you gather there with other kids, start working together. Use your cards and tape to create a model of a church building.**

Stand in the middle of the activity area. Begin reading from the cards, one at a time. Someone who has that skill will run past you, take the card, and go to the other side of the room. If two or more kids run past you for the same card, have the kids run in place briefly as you hand out additional blank cards.

As kids reach the other side of the room, they'll use their index cards and tape to build a model church building. Kids with a blank index card can use the pencil to write their talent on their note card. When everyone's at the other side of the room and working together to create their church structure, ask:

We Can Do It

continued

TIP When listing skills and talents, be realistic for kids' age. For example: "I'm good at math," "I'm good at soccer," "I can bake chocolate chip cookies," or "I'm a good listener." Depending on kids' ages and personalities, you might want to include some humorous or gross examples (which kids will love), such as "I can burp louder than anyone else." Also, for some skills that are common or popular, such as "I'm good at math," or "I'm good at video games," make more than one card.

- *Who is good at math?*
- *Who makes good chocolate chip cookies?*
- *Who is good at video games?*
- *Who plays the piano?*

Let kids identify by name their peers who possessed each skill, going through the list of all skills so that by the end, they know each other's names well. Praise the work kids have done on their model church.

· Debrief

After playing, ask kids to sit together for a discussion.

- *Describe activities you like to do by yourself.*
- *Tell about things you like to do with other people.*
- *How can each person's skills or abilities be a good thing for our church?*
- *How can we use our skills to help our church?*

Stationary Soccer

Kids learn about finding God's
direction while playing this game.

AGES 10-12

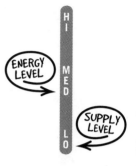

SCRIPTURE

Psalm 37:23-24

SUPPLIES

Bible, two blindfolds

PREPARATION

TIP This game requires large teams of about 10-15 kids and a large area to play.

Have kids form teams of exactly 10 or exactly 15 although you can play this game with more or fewer kids on each team. This game can be played with any number of teams.

Say: **Choose one player on your team to be a human "Soccer Ball" and have him or her come up to get a blindfold. The rest of the team members will spread out in a bowling-pin pattern with two kids in the smallest row. These players will be "Goal Posts."**

Start the point of each bowling-pin pattern with two kids standing about four feet apart. Then have a second row of three kids stand four feet from the first row, and four feet apart from each other. Continue with this spacing for the third row of four kids. If you have 15 kids on each team, add a fourth row of five kids. For smaller teams or teams of odd numbers, decrease rows or number of kids in each row so that everyone is able to play. Always start with two Goal Posts and build up from there.

HUMAN SOCCER BALL

GOAL POSTS

Blindfold each human Soccer Ball, and lead him or her to stand somewhere between the two rows farthest from the Goal Posts (or in the middle of the longer row if you have smaller teams).

Spin each Soccer Ball a few times, and then say: **The object of this game is for one blindfolded human Soccer Ball to score a goal by walking between the two Goal Post players in the shortest row before the other team can get their Soccer Ball into their goal box. No one may talk, but if your Soccer Ball is going to bump into you, you can try to spin him or her toward the right direction. You can only touch your Soccer Ball's arms or shoulders, and only for one second each time. If you touch your Soccer Ball anywhere else or for longer than one second, he or she has to start over from the beginning.**

Answer any questions teams may have about the game before enforcing the silent rule as play starts.

Say: **This is a silent game. From now on, everyone must be completely silent.**

Play several rounds, having teams choose a new Soccer Ball with each round.

- (Debrief) -

At the end of the game, gather kids and read aloud Psalm 37:23-24. Then discuss the following.

- *What helped you—and what didn't help—in this game?*
- *Tell about a time you had difficulty knowing what to do.*
- *How can God give you direction when you need help?*

Say: **When you're lost and need direction, remember to ask God for wisdom and guidance.**

True Servants

Kids discover how they can serve
their friends and neighbors.

AGES 10-12

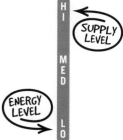

With kids seated in chairs, set your group of items in the middle of the circle.

Say: **One at a time, we're each going to choose one item from the center of the room, and use it in some way to serve someone else in the circle. Let's see if we can come up with some creative ways to serve one another with what we have here.**

Make sure everyone is served at least once.

Afterward, say: **The Bible tells us about a time when Jesus served his disciples.** Read aloud John 13:3-5, 12-17.

Debrief

Discuss the following.

- *Describe what you were thinking when you served others.*
- *What was it like to have others serve you?*
- *Why do you think Jesus served his disciples?*
- *What are ways we can follow Jesus' example and serve other people this week?*

Encourage everyone to follow up on their ideas to serve others during the week. Remember to ask for reports at your next gathering.

SCRIPTURE

John 13:3-5, 12-17

SUPPLIES

Bible; chairs; a group of items such as a pencil, sheet of paper, string, roll of tape, empty cup, towel, water bottle, eraser, and so on (there should be at least one item per child)

PREPARATION

Arrange a circle of chairs for kids to sit in.

TOPIC
Serving

Best for

AGES 10-12

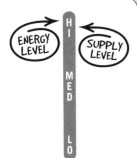

SCRIPTURE

Matthew 25:34-36

 SUPPLIES

Bible; station instructions written on index cards; and one of the following for each group of six kids: small boxes of crackers, blindfolds, large bandages, coats, hats, paper cups, pitcher of drinking water

 PREPARATION

Set up five stations in your meeting area. Spread out the stations and place brief instructions at each station. At station one, place small boxes of crackers. Put blindfolds at station two and bandages at station three. At station four, place coats and hats. At station five, set out paper cups and a pitcher of drinking water.

ALLERGY ALERT!
See page 8

Seeing Jesus

Kids understand what it means to see Jesus in the less fortunate people of their world.

Separate the group into teams of at least six kids each. If teams aren't equal, some team members will need to take more than one turn.

Say: **Each person on the team will be part of a relay. One person from each team will be stationed as the "Host" at each of the five stations. The remaining people on the team are the "Runners," going from station to station.**

At the first station, the first Host will feed the Runner an entire box of crackers. Then the Runner will proceed to the next station, where the second Host will blindfold the Runner and lead him or her to the third station. When they get to the third station, the third Host will wrap the Runner with a bandage. Since the Runner is now blindfolded and wrapped in a bandage, the third Host will guide him or her to the next station, where the fourth Host will help the Runner put on a coat and hat. Finally, the Runner will be escorted to station five, where the fifth Host will pour a cup of water and hold it for the Runner to drink all of the water.

Start the relay. Continue play until all teams finish, then say: **The stations in this relay come from a passage in the Bible.**

Read aloud Matthew 25:34-36.

Debrief

At the end of the game, discuss the following.

- *Why can it seem difficult to help people in need?*
- *What can we do more to be sensitive to the needs of those around us?*
- *Tell about a person in need (no names) whom you could help this week.*
- *Explain how we can "see Jesus" in people who are in need.*

Say: **Even though we raced each other, we all win when we serve and love people like Jesus tells us to do.**

Ultimate Consequence

AGES 10-12

Best for

Kids will build a cross for themselves and discover that Jesus accepted the ultimate consequence—by taking their place.

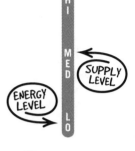

Say: **Today you're going to build a cross for yourself.**

Form groups of three, and give each group one die and 20 strips of paper per child. Ask each group to choose one player to begin the game.

Say: **The first player will roll the die and write one sin on that number of paper strips. That player will lay those strips on the floor, starting to create a cross that is the same size as the tallest person in your group. The tallest person in your group can lie on the floor and spread out his or her arms to show the group how large to make the cross.** The game continues as each player rolls the die and builds the group's cross with the paper strips.

When everyone has finished, read aloud Galatians 6:7-8 and John 19:17-18.

Then say: **The consequence of our sin is death. We all deserve to die because of our sin. But God loves us so much that he sent his Son, Jesus, to die in our place on a cross. Jesus accepted the consequence of our sin.** Encourage kids to tear up their paper crosses and thank Jesus for dying in their place.

 SCRIPTURE

Galatians 6:7-8;
John 19:17-18

 SUPPLIES

Bible, scissors, colored construction paper, one die for every three kids

 PREPARATION

Cut the construction paper into 20 one-inch strips per child.

· Debrief · ·

At the end of the game, discuss the following.

- *What were you thinking as you were building a cross with your group?*
- *What were you thinking when you tore up the cross?*
- *Even though Jesus paid the price for our sins, what are some consequences we still might face when we do wrong things?*

Say: **God is a forgiving God. But sin can still have severe consequences that affect us and others. Even so, when we sin we can ask God for forgiveness immediately. Because of Jesus, God will forgive us.**

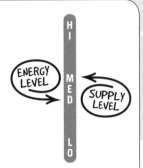

Best for

AGES 10-12

SCRIPTURE

Ruth 2:8-12

SUPPLIES

Bible; one roll of pennies; one of the following for every two kids: small plastic resealable bag, one clean cloth blindfold

PREPARATION

Clear the center of your area of obstacles, and sprinkle pennies all over the floor.

Grain Game

Kids experience how Ruth trusted God to take care of her and how they can trust God, too.

Once the group divides into pairs, give each pair a blindfold.

Say: **In the Bible, Ruth had to go to the fields to glean, or gather, grain. She had to trust God to help her find enough grain so she and Naomi would have food. In this game, you and your partner will have to trust each other in order to gather "grain." Pennies will represent grain.**

Tell partners to decide who'll be the "Gleaner" and who'll be the "Director." Each Gleaner will wear the blindfold and hold a plastic bag.

Say: **On my signal, the Gleaners will drop to their knees and await instructions from the Directors. The Directors can tell the Gleaners where the "grain" is and how to avoid other Gleaners, but they can't touch the Gleaners at any point.**

Let the Gleaners gather grain for several minutes, then call time. The Gleaners can show their bags to their partners, then sprinkle the pennies on the floor again. Have partners switch roles and play again. After calling time again, work together to clean up all the pennies from the floor. Put the pennies in the offering.

Debrief

At the end of the game, discuss the following.

* *Describe how it felt to trust your partner to tell you where the grain was.*

Read aloud Ruth 2:8-12.

* *How is our experience like or unlike how Ruth had to trust God to give her enough grain for food?*
* *Tell about a time it was difficult for you to trust God.*
* *How can Ruth's situation remind you of God's care for you?*

Encourage kids to remember how God took care of Ruth and assure them that they, too, can trust God in every situation.

Are You Asking for It?

Kids attempt a challenge and learn why it's important to ask for God's help.

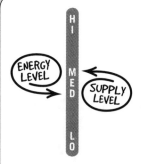

SCRIPTURE
Judges 6:33-40

SUPPLIES
Bible, timer or stopwatch, masking tape

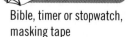
PREPARATION
none

Say: **God gave a man named Gideon a difficult and important task. Gideon had to lead the Israelites to victory over the Midianites. He asked God questions so he'd know what to do, and he asked God for help so he could correctly do the job God had for him.**

Ask kids to talk about situations when they had to do something difficult and needed God's help. Be ready with an appropriate example from your life.

Have kids pair up and give one child from each pair a strip of masking tape. Then say: **Let's do something challenging now. Stick your masking tape on your partner's back between his or her shoulders.** Allow time. **The partner with the tape will have 30 seconds to try to get the piece of tape off—without using his or her hands. Ready, go!**

Allow time. If no one discovers the secret to the game (asking the partner to pull off the tape), play again, this time with the partners swapping roles.

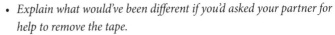

After the game, ask:

- *What was this game like for you?*
- *Explain what would've been different if you'd asked your partner for help to remove the tape.*
- *Why do you think it's important to ask for God's help when we face challenges in real life?*

Say: **I challenged you by saying you couldn't touch the tape—and then I waited to see whether you'd ask your partner to help rather than trying to do it yourself. God doesn't play games like this with us, but he does want us to ask for his help when we need it.**

Gideon knew he needed God's help. Sometimes we forget to ask for God's help. When we face difficulties, we don't have to rely on our own strength; we can get help from our great God. Anytime you need it, you can ask God for help.

AGES 10-12

Overflowing Oil

Kids experience the excitement of gathering an abundance of oil.

Read aloud 2 Kings 4:1-7.

Say: **Your goal in this game is to try to collect as much "oil" as you can—in the form of paper wads—in one minute.**

Form groups of three or four, and give each group one bag, their "oil jar." Toss wadded paper all over the room. Tell kids they'll have one minute (or less, if you choose) to collect as much "oil" (paper wads) as they can. Say **"Go!"** and start timing.

As groups collect, have adult volunteers toss out more and more wadded paper so there's always extra to collect. When time's up, shout **"Stop!"** Encourage players to give others in their group and everyone else high fives, congratulations, and positive words for their hard work.

Debrief

When the game is over, form a large group and discuss the following.

- *Explain what it was like to try to fill up your "oil jar" (your bag) before time was up.*
- *Explain why you think the woman in this Scripture was blessed.*
- *How does God bless you and your family?*

Say: **When we tell God about what we need, sometimes God gives us even more than we expect!**

SCRIPTURE

2 Kings 4:1-7

SUPPLIES

Bible, garbage bags or paper or plastic grocery bags (one per three or four kids), lots of wadded newspaper or scrap paper, timer or stopwatch, one or two adult volunteers

PREPARATION

Wad up many pieces of newspaper or scrap paper.

AGES 10-12

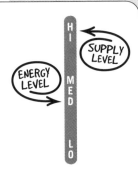

SCRIPTURE

John 4:7-14

SUPPLIES

Bible; timer or stopwatch; towel; one cup of water, and one drinking straw per person

PREPARATION

Running on Thirsty

Kids transfer water in a unique way and discuss how Jesus quenches our thirst.

Ask kids to stand against one wall, and give everyone a straw. Place cups with water on the ground near each child, while placing empty cups on the floor about 10 feet away. Demonstrate how to hold water in the straw by dipping it in the cup, plugging the top with a finger, and lifting the straw. On "Go!" give kids 60 seconds to see how much water they can transfer to their empty cups using only their straws.

Debrief

When time's up, read aloud John 4:7-14. Then sit together and discuss the following.

- *Tell about a time you were really thirsty and how you quenched your thirst.*

Say: **The woman drew water at the well, just like you drew water with your straws. Jesus, though, talked about a different kind of water.**

Ask:

- *What was the "water" Jesus talked about?*
- *What kinds of "thirsts" do you think Jesus' water could quench?*

Hold up a cup of water and say: **Just like the water the woman got out of the well, the water in this cup will run out—but Jesus' living water never runs out!**

AGES 10-12

Keep Your Focus

Kids play a blindfold game to encourage
them to stay focused on God.

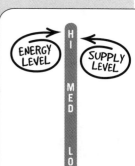

SCRIPTURE

Hebrews 11:1-3

SUPPLIES

Bible; timer or
stopwatch; lots of cotton
balls, two plastic bowls,
blindfold, chair, and
plastic spoon per person

Begin with half of the kids seated in chairs. Place one bowl in each child's lap and one on his or her head (kids can use their hand to hold the bowl on their head if needed). Fill the lap bowls with cotton balls. Hand the kids a spoon, then blindfold them. Give them one minute to spoon as many cotton balls as possible from their lap bowls into their head bowls.

Invite the rest of the group to shout out encouragement or distractions. Kids may even shout wrong directions, but they can't touch the kids or blow on the cotton balls. After one minute, call time and applaud the kids. Continue until everyone's had a turn.

PREPARATION

Afterward, gather everyone together and discuss the following.

- *Why was this game a challenge for you?*
- *How was this experience like or unlike challenges of having faith in real life?*

Say: **You had faith that the two bowls were where they were supposed to be, even though you couldn't see them. To have faith means to believe in something you can't see. And sometimes, even though you have faith, you may mess up like you did in this game. The important thing is to keep your focus on God and believe what he tells you, no matter what.**

The Bible gives us lots of examples of faithful people to encourage us. Read aloud Hebrews 11:1-3. Then read several verses of your choice in that chapter to give examples of what it means to be faithful to God. (Noah, Abraham, and Moses are people that kids are probably familiar with and they are mentioned in the chapter.)

Best for

AGES 10-12

ENERGY LEVEL

SUPPLY LEVEL

HI MED LO

SCRIPTURE

John 20:24-31

SUPPLIES

Bible

PREPARATION

I Doubt It!

kids discover that Jesus accepts us, even if we sometimes have doubts.

Organize everyone into groups of four. Explain that kids will each think of three statements about themselves. Two statements should be true, and one should be invented. Group members will try to guess which statements are true and which aren't. If kids doubt a statement, they'll jump up and say, "I doubt it!" After everyone has expressed an opinion, the speaker will reveal which statement was invented.

Debrief

After everyone has had a turn, discuss the following.

- *Describe what it's like trying to decide if something was true or not.*
- *How do you know whether to believe what people say?*

Say: **There's a passage in the Bible about a man who didn't believe what his friends were saying.**

Open your Bible to John 20:24-31, and summarize the passage.

Say: **After Jesus came back to life, people began seeing him. But some people doubted that Jesus had overcome death, including his disciple, Thomas. Thomas even said, "I won't believe it unless I see the nail wounds in his hands, put my fingers into them, and place my hand into the wound in his side." Not long after that, Jesus appeared to his disciples, including Thomas, and said, "Put your finger here, and look at my hands. Put your hand into the wound in my side. Don't be faithless any longer. Believe!" And Thomas stopped doubting.**

Ask for responses to the following.

- *Why do you think Thomas doubted that Jesus was alive?*
- *Tell about a time you had doubts about God and what you did about those doubts.*
- *Why do you think Jesus accepts us, even though we sometimes doubt?*

AGES 10-12

Greased Pig

Kids discover what it means
to "hold tight" to God's promises.

ENERGY LEVEL

SUPPLY LEVEL

HI
MED
LO

 SCRIPTURE

Hebrews 10:23-25

Greet children as they arrive, and say: **I want you to "grease up" using the baby oil to make your hands slick.** Give the same treatment to a foam football to make catching the ball especially tricky.

 SUPPLIES

Bible, one foam football per 12 kids, a bottle of baby oil, roll of paper towels, rags and a bucket of soapy water (optional)

Say: **Let's form a large circle and pass the ball around and across the circle, counting tosses to see how long we can keep the ball in the air without dropping it.**

Play several rounds so that everyone has plenty of opportunities to try their slippery hand at the ball. For larger groups, play with more than one greasy football.

After playing this game and cleaning up, have kids sit down together. Read aloud Hebrews 10:23-25.

 PREPARATION

This game will be messy, so encourage kids beforehand to dress in play clothes, and secure an outdoor location for game play. You may want to have rags and a bucket of soapy water on hand for easy cleanup.

Debrief

Discuss the following.

- *Explain what made this game easy or difficult.*
- *Tell about a time in life when it was difficult for you to hold on to hope.*
- *Why is it sometimes challenging to remember what God has in store for you?*
- *Why can you hold on to the hope God gives you?*

Close by reminding kids to hang on tight to God's promises and not drop the ball when trouble comes.

Best for

AGES 10-12

SCRIPTURE

Proverbs 31:25-27

SUPPLIES

Bible, mouse pad, spatula, clean sock or T-shirt, stuffed animal

PREPARATION

Mom's Typical Day

Kids appreciate the many ways that their mothers or other important women help them.

Bring one willing child to the center of your room to play the "Mother." Then form four relay teams (Team A, Team B, and so on), and direct each team to a different corner of the room. Give one team the mouse pad, one team a spatula, another team a sock or T-shirt, and the last team a stuffed animal.

Say: **Each of these objects represents some of the things moms do on a daily basis—working, cooking, cleaning, and taking care of pets. That's a lot to do! When I say, "Happy Mother's Day!" the first person on each team will toss his or her object to our Mother and run to the back of the line. Our Mother will catch or pick up these objects and toss them randomly to the four teams. For example, if Mother catches the spatula from Team A, she could toss it to Team D. Mother will be busily trying to catch and throw the objects at all times. The next person on each team will then throw his or her object to our Mother, and repeat until everyone has thrown and caught an object.**

Say **"Happy Mother's Day!"** to begin the game. After one minute, switch roles so someone else is Mother. Play a few times.

Debrief

At the end of the game, ask:

- *If you were Mother, what was it like trying to catch and throw all these objects?*
- *How is this like a mother trying to handle a busy day?*
- *If you were a thrower, how does this game make you think of all that your mom does for you?*

Read aloud Proverbs 31:25-27.

- *What's one way you can show thanks to your mother this week?*

AGES 10-12

Dark and Stormy Night

Kids consider why Jesus understands when we're afraid.

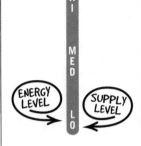

SCRIPTURE

Psalm 27:1-2

SUPPLIES

Bible, paper, pencil

PREPARATION

Tell kids they're bestselling authors of scary mystery stories. Choose someone to start, and give him or her paper and a pencil. Explain that kids will write a scary mystery story together.

The person with the paper and pencil will create the title of a story. Then have that person pass the paper and pencil to somenoe else. Have the second person add a sentence to the story. Continue passing the paper and pencil until everyone has had a chance to add a sentence to the story. Then choose somebody to read the entire story aloud to the group.

Debrief

Afterward, discuss the following.

- *Explain what it was like to add your part to our story, but not know how it would end.*
- *We made up a scary story for fun. What things are you afraid of in real life?*

Read aloud Psalm 27:1-2.

- *Why do you think Jesus understands when we're afraid?*
- *How can Jesus help calm our fears?*

Say: **Jesus was fully God and fully human, so he knows what it's like to be afraid. He understands how each of us feels when we are afraid, and he's always there to listen to us and help us feel better.**

Best for

AGES 10-12

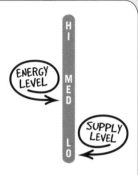

SCRIPTURE

Psalm 23:1-4

SUPPLIES

Bible, large collection of various objects (just about anything will do)

PREPARATION

Form two piles of various objects at one end of the room.

Comfort Relay

Kids consider how Jesus comforts them.

Designate two teams, each facing one of the piles of objects.

Say: **I'll describe a situation in which a person might need comfort. For each situation, your team will send one person down to the team's pile of objects to find something that would bring comfort in that situation and bring it back. Then the team will say how that thing could bring comfort.**

Call out one of the following scenarios:

- *You're stranded on a desert island.*
- *You forgot to bring your lunch to school.*
- *You got caught in a sudden rainstorm.*
- *You missed the bus to get home.*
- *You've been attacked by a ferocious band of ducks.*
- *You've fallen into a giant vat of honey.*

Ask each team to explain how its chosen item would bring comfort. Then keep playing, with teams choosing new representatives each time.

Debrief

At the end of the game, discuss the following.

- *Why do people need comfort at times?*
- *What are ways that people try to comfort themselves?*
- *How does Jesus comfort us?*

Say: **We can take comfort in any situation by knowing that God cares for us and watches over us.** Close by reading aloud Psalm 23:1-4.

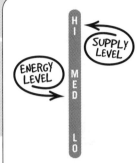

Best for

AGES 10-12

Balloon Bust

Kids discover the "fairness" of Jesus' death for our sins.

SUPPLY LEVEL

ENERGY LEVEL

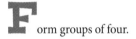

Form groups of four.

Say: **I'm going to dump balloons on the floor. When I say "Go!" you'll begin stomping on the balloons to make them pop. Make sure to check the balloons after you pop them because some contain strips of paper that are worth points. Your group will have to earn a certain number of points to get a snack.**

Dump the balloons on the floor and let kids begin.

After all of the balloons are popped, have kids return to their groups.

Say: **The white strips are worth two points, the green strips are worth four points, and the blue strips are worth six points. Add up your points and tell the rest of us how many points your group earned.**

Announce that they must have one or more points to win the snack, and distribute the snack to everyone.

Debrief

At the end of the game, discuss the following.

- *Explain whether you were worried that you might not get a snack.*
- *What were you thinking when you found out everyone got a snack?*
- *How is this experience like or unlike how our faith in Jesus saves us?*
- *Explain whether you think it's fair that everyone who believes in Jesus will have eternal life.*

Say: **In our game, no matter how many points you had, it was enough. No matter how good we are, we still need Jesus to be able to go to heaven.**

SCRIPTURE

Ephesians 2:8-9

SUPPLIES

Bible; balloons; white, green, and blue strips of paper; garbage bags; snacks

PREPARATION

Place one strip of paper in half of the balloons, and inflate two balloons for each person. Put the balloons in garbage bags for easy handling.

BALLOON WARNING! See page 8

ALLERGY ALERT! See page 8

AGES 10-12

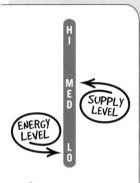

Prosthetic Noses

Kids use this crazy contest for an unforgettable lesson on being honest about who we are.

SCRIPTURE

1 Samuel 16:7

SUPPLIES

Bible, mirrors, Silly Putty or bubble gum for each child

PREPARATION

Consider making a certificate for the contest winner by cutting pictures of noses from magazines and taping them to a page that reads "Best Prosthetic Nose Award."

ALLERGY ALERT!
See page 8

Say: **It's time for a makeover. I want you to give yourself a nose job using these supplies.**

Let kids go to work molding the putty on their noses to create a new look. Bubble gum could be used as an economical, albeit more messy, substitution. If using bubble gum, have kids each chew their gum and then mold it on their own noses. Give kids a few minutes to complete their noses.

Afterward, ask players to vote for the nose they like best.

Debrief

At the end of the game, discuss the following.

- *What was it like to create a new nose for yourself?*
- *How do these noses create a different image of your face?*
- *What are other ways we portray a "false image" of who we are inside?*

Read aloud 1 Samuel 16:7.

- *Why do you think it matters to God whether we are honest about who we really are or if we portray a false image?*

Say: **It's fun creating new noses. But it's easy to create a false image of ourselves in other ways. Remember, God wants us to be honest about who we really are, both to others and ourselves. After all, God made each of us and values us all equally.**

Faith Commitment

AGES 10-12

Wiggle-Waggle

kids discover that no matter how many times we mess up, God still forgives us.

SCRIPTURE

Proverbs 2:20

SUPPLIES

Bible

PREPARATION

Practice doing the Wiggle-Waggle with your hands before trying to teach kids how to do it.

Say: **I'm going to teach you some hand motions today. It's just a matter of rotating your hands in the proper direction.**

Walk through the following instructions slowly with kids, ensuring everyone makes it through the step-by-step instructions and ends up with their hands in the proper positions.

Say:

1. **Put your hands in front of your face, palm to palm, then cross your middle fingers.**

2. **After crossing your middle fingers, if your *left* middle finger is closer to you, rotate your *right* palm outward and away from you and your *left* fingers behind your *right* palm. If your *right* middle finger is closer to you, rotate your *left* palm outward and away from you and your *right* fingers behind your *left* palm.**

3. **After you rotate, your middle fingers should be opposite from one another. None of your other fingers should cross over each other, and your thumbs should touch your pinky fingers. Position your hands parallel to the ground with one middle finger pointing up in the air while the other is pointing down.**

4. **Now wiggle and waggle your middle fingers.**

Let kids practice until they get more familiar with the motions, and then ask them to find partners.

Say: **Now you must do the Wiggle-Waggle with each other. To do this, you'll stand face-to-face, palm-to-palm with one another, and rotate to the wiggle-waggle position.**

Next, have players form a circle with their hands at their sides. When you say "Go!" have kids do the Wiggle-Waggle with the people on their left and right simultaneously. After 15 seconds say **"Stop!"** After three attempts, ask the kids whether they'd evaluate their efforts as a success or a failure. (Because of the complexity of this exercise, most will feel like they failed or did the steps wrong.)

· (Debrief) ·

At the end of the game, discuss the following.

- *Explain how you felt about this challenge.*
- *Even though we walked through the instructions, most of you didn't do it right in the challenge. Explain why.*

Read aloud Proverbs 2:20.

- *How was this experience like or unlike when we don't do the right thing in real life?*
- *When we make mistakes, how can we get back on the right path?*

Say: **Even though we sometimes fail, God never fails us. He's always with us, always ready to guide us back to the right path.**

AGES 10-12

Fifteen-Ball

Kids discover that finding wisdom
starts with looking up.

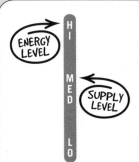

SCRIPTURE

Isaiah 55:8-9

SUPPLIES

Bible, one inflated beach
ball, one long rope, two
supports between which
the rope may be tied
(trees, poles, or walls)

PREPARATION

Tie a rope horizontally
between two supports
15 feet above the ground
(lower if your group is
younger).

Hold up an inflated beach ball and say: **The object of this game is to hit this ball over the rope and end up with 15 points. You get one point every time the ball goes over the rope, unless you kick it over or hit it over with your head. You're all on the same team and can play any position you like. In fact, I encourage you to change sides by moving back and forth under the rope.**

Here are a few more rules: You can hit the ball as many times as you'd like before you get it over the rope, but the same person can't hit it twice in a row. If the ball hits the ground, you lose all the points. You can't catch the ball, but you can hit, smack, or kick it with any part of your body. If it seems helpful, encourage kids not to get too rough as they play the game.

After the team scores 15 points, gather kids in a circle.

Debrief

After the game, discuss:

- *What was playing this game like for you?*
- *What was easy or difficult about scoring 15 points?*

Read aloud Isaiah 55:8-9.

- *What do you think this Scripture means when it says God's ways are higher than our ways and God's thoughts are higher than our thoughts?*
- *In this game, you had to keep looking up to score points. Plus, you had lots of ways to score points. How is this like what happens when we focus on following God?*
- *Why do you think God makes it easy for us to be his friend?*

Play the game again. Each time the ball goes over the high rope, have everyone shout, "Look up!"

Best for

AGES 10-12

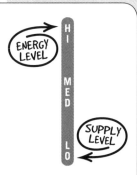

Fly So High

Kids discover the power of prayer.

SCRIPTURE

Revelation 8:4-5

SUPPLIES

Bible, tissues (or anything that floats in air)

PREPARATION

Have children form teams of four.

Say: **Listen to a verse that talks about our prayers ascending, or going up, to God.**

Read aloud Revelation 8:4-5; then say: **Let's see what upward floating prayers might look like!**

Give each team a tissue.

Say: **Teams will have to work together to get the tissue to touch the ceiling. You can't use your hands; you must make the tissue rise by blowing on it.**

When one team's tissue touches the ceiling, let kids catch their breath and then sit in a circle.

Debrief

At the end of the game, discuss the following.

- *How are the floating tissues like prayer? How are they different?*
- *How can it help to ask others to join us in prayer help when we have a problem?*

Say: **Our prayers go up to God, and he hears them! We can talk to God anytime, and we know he'll answer.**

Following Jesus

Backward Bonanza

AGES 10-12

Kids play games backward to help them remember one of Jesus' teachings.

Say: **You've all been selected to compete in an unusual event: the Backward Bonanza. Every game we play will be played backward!**

Form groups of four, and let kids try these backward events:

- Say the alphabet as quickly as possible—backward!

- Run a relay race—backward!

- Walk a line without looking behind them—backward!

- Toss and catch balls to each other—backward!

Debrief

Afterward, discuss the following.

- *What was it like to play these games backward?*

Say: **Sometimes in real life, we're asked to do things that may seem backward at first. Listen to what Jesus said.** Read aloud Matthew 16:24-26.

Ask:

- *What do you think Jesus meant when he said that to save your life, you must give it up to him?*
- *Explain whether you think that Jesus' instructions feel backward.*

Say: **Jesus said that to be his follower, we have to act in ways that may seem backward at first. But he's there to help us. He'll help us follow him. And that's not backward at all!**

SCRIPTURE

Matthew 16:24-26

SUPPLIES

Bible

PREPARATION

Best for

AGES 10-12

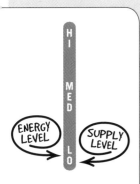

SCRIPTURE

Acts 9:11-19

SUPPLIES

Bible, toothpicks

PREPARATION

What's Changed?

Kids will guess changes that have been made
and learn that God changes hearts.

Ask kids to form groups of four, and give each group an equal number of toothpicks. Each group will create a design on a table with toothpicks. When groups have finished making their designs, tell kids to look closely at their designs so they can remember what they look like.

Then have groups move so they're looking at another group's design.

Say: **Your job now is to make one change to the design in front of you. You can't mess up the design, though. Make a change you think the other group won't notice right away.**

After groups have made changes, have them go back to their original designs. Have each group try to guess what the change was. The group who made the change can confirm or deny the change.

Debrief

After groups have identified all the changes, ask:

- *What was easy or difficult about this experience?*
- *What kinds of changes were easiest to notice? Which were most difficult?*

Say: **We all go through changes in our lives. But when we believe in Jesus, he changes us in drastic ways. Listen to what the Bible says about a man who changed dramatically when he met Jesus.** Read aloud Acts 9:11-19.

Ask for responses to these prompts:

- *How did Jesus change Saul's heart?*
- *How has knowing Jesus changed your heart?*

Say: **When we believe in Jesus, our hearts change forever. Let's say a prayer to show how thankful we are that God changes hearts.** Close with a prayer thanking Jesus for changing your hearts.

AGES 10-12

Forgiveness Freeze Tag

Kids learn what it's like to be set free.

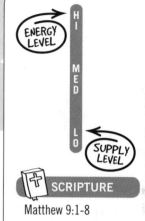

SCRIPTURE

Matthew 9:1-8

SUPPLIES

Bible, cone markers

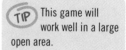
PREPARATION

Use the cones to mark off a playing field.

TIP This game will work well in a large open area.

Choose one person to be the "Healer." Designate one-third of the kids to be "Paralyzers," and tell the rest that they're "Paralytics." Explain that the Paralytics have to make it from one end of the field to the other without getting tagged by a Paralyzer. If they're tagged, they have to freeze. Once frozen, the only way for a Paralytic to move again is for the Healer to touch the person.

Have the Paralytics go to one end of the field and have the Paralyzers go to the middle. The Healer will wander throughout the field.

Debrief

After a few rounds, gather kids together. Read aloud Matthew 9:1-8. Then ask:

- *What could you do to get help if you were paralyzed?*
- *How was the Healer in our game like Jesus?*
- *In what ways does Jesus heal us today?*

Say: **In this Scripture, Jesus healed the paralytic by saying, "Your sins are forgiven!" That wasn't enough for some people. They thought he was saying something he didn't have the authority to say. So Jesus said, "Stand up, pick up your mat, and go home," and the man did. Then the people in the crowd knew Jesus had the authority to heal sins. Jesus can heal your body. But more importantly, Jesus can heal your heart.**

Best for

AGES 10-12

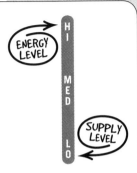
ENERGY LEVEL

HI
MED
LO

SUPPLY LEVEL

SCRIPTURE

Romans 15:5-7

SUPPLIES

Bible, soccer ball

PREPARATION

Left Out

Exclusion helps kids learn how important it is to include others.

Have kids form a circle. Ask the child wearing the most white to step outside the circle. Place the soccer ball in the hands of a child who's in the circle.

Say: **We're going to play a game of Keep Away. Everyone in the circle will pass the ball to someone else in the circle, while the person outside the circle tries to tag someone who is holding the ball. If you're holding the ball and you get tagged, you have to trade places with the person outside the circle. Ready? Go!**

Play until several kids have had a chance to be the person outside the circle.

Debrief

After several rounds, ask:

- *How was this game like or unlike what sometimes happens to kids?*
- *Why do you think we sometimes try to keep others outside our circles?*
- *Why is it important to show love for others like Jesus did by including everyone?*

Gift-Bow Giveaway

Kids will give away bows, not expecting any gifts in return.

AGES 10-12

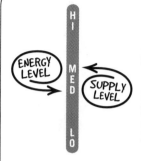

Give each child six gift bows, and have kids stick the bows onto their clothing.

Say: **When I say, "Give a gift!" try to give away your bows by attaching them to other people's clothing—they have to stick. The object is to keep giving away your gift bows so you don't keep any. Ready? Give a gift!**

Debrief

Stop after a few minutes, and gather kids in a circle. Ask:

- *Describe what it was like for you to give away your gift bows in this game.*
- *What kind of gifts do you give in real life?*

Read aloud 2 Corinthians 9:6-7; then ask:

- *What does this passage tell us about giving?*
- *What can you give to God to show him you love him?*

Bring out the bag of snacks with a gift bow on it. Pass around the bag. Ask kids each to take a snack and give it to someone sitting by them. When everyone has a snack, eat and enjoy. Say: **You are gifts to me! Our good God has blessed us with many gifts. Let's always be generous and give cheerfully to others.**

SCRIPTURE

2 Corinthians 9:6-7

SUPPLIES

Bible, gift bows, bag of snacks

PREPARATION

Place a gift bow on the snack bag.

ALLERGY ALERT!
See page 8

Best for

AGES 10-12

Racing Against Circumstance

Kids try to complete a race with constantly changing circumstances.

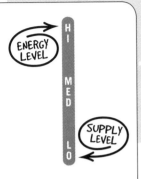
ENERGY LEVEL

HI
MED
LO

SUPPLY LEVEL

SCRIPTURE
Philippians 4:10-13

SUPPLIES
Bible, a cotton ball

PREPARATION
none

Begin by forming teams of no more than five, and have members of each team choose one person from their team to be the Leader. Give each Leader a cotton ball, and move the Leaders to one side of the room. Tell Leaders that their goal is to blow the cotton ball to the other side of the room and back. The teammates' job is to create a changing "circumstance" around their Leader as he or she progresses.

Say: **I'll call out a change of circumstance, and it's the team's job to make the new circumstance real for the Leader. For example, I might call out "earthquake," which means you'd gently shake the Leader as he or she tries to blow the cotton ball across the room.**

Once kids understand, get everyone into position and start the race. As the Leaders move the cotton ball across the floor, call out these changing circumstances (along with the explanations when necessary):

- **A windstorm hits.** (Team members blow on the cotton ball.)
- **An earthquake strikes.** (Team members gently shake the Leader.)
- **An angry mob surrounds the leader.** (Team members form a circle around the Leader.)
- **A car wreck closes the highway.** (Team members form a human roadblock.)

Continue changing the circumstances until someone finishes the race.

Debrief

At the end of the game, say: **Our attitudes don't have to reflect our circumstances. There's a good example in the book of Philippians.** Have a willing child read aloud Philippians 4:10-13. Then discuss the following.

- *Explain how the circumstances in this game affected our attitudes.*
- *In what ways did the Leaders' attitudes affect their actions?*
- *How does a bad attitude affect your ability to do something?*
- *What can we learn from Paul's attitude?*

Say: **Like Paul, God's people can be positive and joyful in the way they approach every challenge in life.**

Best for

AGES 10-12

Goal Tenders

Kids discover God's plan for our lives takes persistence and dedication to his teachings.

SCRIPTURE

Philippians 3:12-14

SUPPLIES

Bible, plastic bowls, buttons

PREPARATION

Divide the class into trios, and give each trio an empty bowl and a handful of buttons.

Say: **January 1 is the first day of the new year. On New Year's Day, many people set goals they'd like to achieve in the coming year.**

Hold up an empty bowl.

Say: **This bowl reminds me of an empty new year, ready to be filled with new experiences, activities, and people. Let's pretend your buttons represent all those fun things. Your goal is to toss your buttons into the empty bowl from three feet away.**

Debrief

After two minutes, stop play and discuss:

• *Explain whether you were able to achieve your goal and pop a button into the bowl each time.*

Say: **In life, sometimes you have to try several times to achieve your goals. But God gives us each a special goal to strive for every day, week, month, and year. Listen to what that goal is.**

Read aloud Philippians 3:12-14. Say: **Our goal is to become what God wants us to be. We can't achieve that in one year. We always keep striving toward the goal.**

Place a bowl in the middle of the group. Say: **As we close, toss a button into this bowl. When you do, think of one way you'll try to become what God wants you to be. Maybe you'll think of reading your Bible, praying, singing songs to God, or showing love and kindness to others. Remember to strive for that goal every day, week, month, and year.**

AGES 10-12

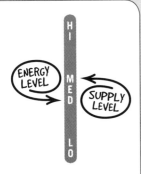

Are You Up to the Challenge?

Kids understand that God's Word challenges each of us to become who God wants us to be.

SCRIPTURE

Psalm 119:9-16

SUPPLIES

Bible, scissors, long piece of rope or twine

PREPARATION

Prepare a simple obstacle course. Keep in mind that kids will travel the course while tied together.

Begin by having kids stand shoulder to shoulder in a circle. Cut a piece of twine or rope that's long enough to stretch around their backs. Then have kids take two steps toward the center of the circle. When they're as close together as they can be, wrap the rope or twine around their backs and tie it so they are all attached as a group. Explain you'll lead the way as they move through an obstacle course. They'll stay tied together the entire time. Remind kids to be careful so no one trips.

Show kids how to move through the obstacle course, giving demonstrations of any complicated obstacles.

Debrief

When kids have completed the course, untie the group. Read aloud Psalm 119:9-16. Then discuss the following questions.

- *What was it like to do this obstacle course while you were all tied together?*
- *How did you have to change your usual behavior to complete this challenge?*
- *How is this challenge like or unlike the commandments God gives us to follow in the Bible?*

Say: **Just as we were challenged during this obstacle course, God gives us commands to follow in the Bible. He wants us to become more like him as we cooperate with his purposes in our lives. And just as we worked together to solve our challenge today, God gives us support and guidance in his Word to help us.**

Valentine's Day

God's Heart for You

Kids contemplate several ways that God loves them.

AGES 10-12

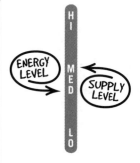

Read aloud John 3:16-17. Say: **God showed his special love for us when he sent his Son, Jesus. There's no better Valentine than that!**

Give each person a copy of the "God's Love Is for YOU!" handout (found at the end of the Upper Elementary section) and a pen.

Show kids a candy heart and say: **These candy hearts have little sayings**

God's Love Is for YOU!

Permission to photocopy this handout from The Giant Book of Games for Children's Ministry granted for local church use.
Copyright © Group Publishing, Inc., 1515 Cascade Ave., Loveland, CO 80538. group.com

on them to show appreciation or love. As fun as it is to receive these words, we have a better way to receive love. Each of you will go up to as many people as possible and write one way God loves that person on his or her heart paper. For example, you could write "God created you in a special way."

While you're writing on someone's heart, that person will also write on yours. Let's see how many people we can share God's love with!

Set a time limit based on how many kids you have. Allow two minutes for every 10 kids.

SCRIPTURE

John 3:16-17

SUPPLIES

Bible, "God's Love Is for You!" handout (at the end of the Upper Elementary section), pens, timer or stopwatch, conversation heart candies

PREPARATION

Copy one "God's Love Is for You!" handout for each player. (Handout is found at the end of the Upper Elementary section of Games.)

ALLERGY ALERT!
See page 8

········· Debrief ·········

When time is up, share the candies with everyone. Then discuss the following together.

- *Explain what this experience was like for you—both giving and receiving love.*
- *How is God's love for you the ultimate valentine?*

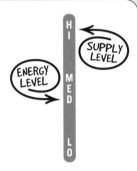

Best for

AGES 10-12

 SCRIPTURE

Isaiah 6:1-8

 SUPPLIES

Bible; kitchen tongs (one set per three to six kids); small cube-shaped items such as dice, blocks, and so on (two to four per player); empty shoe box

 PREPARATION

Burning Coal Bustle

Kids discover God's power and forgiveness as they learn about Isaiah's vision of God.

Read aloud Isaiah 6:1-8. Explain that kids will carry blocks with tongs the same way a seraph carried a burning coal to purify Isaiah when he saw the Lord. Scatter blocks (or dice) at one end of the play area. Explain that the blocks will be "burning coals" and the kids are "Seraphim." Have kids stand behind the burning coals. At the other end of the room, place an empty box. Hand out the kitchen tongs. At your signal, the Seraphs carrying tongs will use them to pick up a burning coal. The Seraphs will walk on tiptoe to the box and drop the burning coal into the box.

The Seraphim will duck-walk back to the starting area, jump up and shout "Here I am. Send me." (Isaiah's words) and pass the tongs to another Seraph. Continue until all the burning coals are in the box.

Debrief

When the game is over, ask kids to sit down in groups of three and discuss the following.

- *Why do you think the seraph carried a burning coal to Isaiah and touched his lips?*
- *What, if anything, surprises you about Isaiah's experience?*
- *Why is it important to admit our sins to God so we can share God's message with others?*

Say: **Isaiah was able to volunteer to do God's work because he knew he needed forgiveness from sin and he admitted it to God. God is always ready for us when we need to ask for forgiveness for our sins.**

AGES 10-12

Listen Up!

This game helps kids remember
to listen for the Holy Spirit.

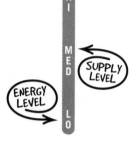

Have kids form pairs. Give each pair a wire clothes hanger and a length of string. Demonstrate how to tie the middle of the string to the hook of the hanger. Show kids how to wrap one end of the string several times around one index finger, and the other end of the string around the other index finger. Indicate how to place the ends of their index fingers lightly in their ears and bend over carefully. Then let the hanger hit lightly against a chair or table. Surprisingly, the sound will be like church bells or an old-fashioned clock.

Ask kids what they think they'll hear when they perform the experiment themselves. Then let partners take turns doing the trick. Challenge kids to see how loud and how quiet they can make the sound.

After everyone has had a turn, collect the supplies.

Debrief

Afterward, ask kids to sit in groups of four and discuss:

- *Explain whether you heard what you expected to hear.*
- *Tell about some unexpected ways God communicates with you.*
- *How can you be more open to hearing and obeying the Holy Spirit?*

Say: **Sometimes God speaks to us in unexpected ways. God sends the Holy Spirit to remind us of what Jesus said, to comfort us, and to help us. We can all be open to hearing what the Holy Spirit has to say.**

SCRIPTURE

John 16:13-15;
Acts 2:1-21

SUPPLIES

Bible, one wire clothes hanger for every two kids, 5-foot length of string for every two kids, chair or table

PREPARATION

AGES 10-12

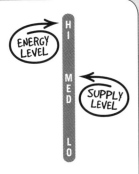

John 8:34-36

Bible, masking tape, blindfolds

Use masking tape to mark off an area that's large enough for your group to comfortably walk around in.

I'm Free

Kids learn about freedom in Jesus.

Choose a willing helper, and ask him or her to put on a blindfold. Form trios, and have everyone step inside the area you've designated for the game. Give each trio a blindfold, and ask them to blindfold one person in their group. Instruct the kids with no blindfolds to face each other and hold hands. The blindfolded kids from each trio will stand between these two kids inside their arms.

Say: **My helper has been freed and is now going to help set others free. Those of you who are holding hands, it's your job to gently guide the person between your hands away from my helper. If my helper tags any of you, the two people who were holding hands must let go and move out of the playing field. The person with the blindfold who was between their arms can then try to set other people free by tagging them.**

If you are tagged and go out of the playing field, help those with blindfolds stay inside it by gently guiding them back in.

Signal for kids to begin the game and help your helper navigate throughout the playing area. Once everyone is free, let kids switch roles and play the game again.

Debrief

At the end of the game, read aloud John 8:34-36. Then discuss the following.

- *Explain what you were thinking when you were trapped between two people's arms.*
- *What was it like to be set free?*
- *How does Jesus set us free?*
- *How can we help set others free?*

AGES 10-12

Belly of the Fish

kids discover how God shows us grace
when we run away from him.

SCRIPTURE

Jonah 1

SUPPLIES

Bible, blindfolds or new rolls of bathroom tissue (optional)

PREPARATION

Move all furniture from the center of the room.

Say: **I need one of you to be a "Fish." The rest of you will be "Jonahs."**

Move kids to the center of the room. Explain that the Fish must open and close his or her mouth by putting his or her arms together and then pulling them apart. The Fish should work to tag the Jonahs. Each time a Jonah gets tagged, the Fish must stop while the new Jonah is blindfolded. The blindfolded Jonah then goes in the belly of the Fish by lining up behind the Fish, placing one hand on his or her shoulder, and using the other hand to try and tag anyone not yet captured. Continue playing until everyone has become part of the Fish.

Debrief

At the end of the game, summarize what happened to Jonah or read the first chapter of the book of Jonah.
Then say: **Jonah thought he could escape his problem by running away—kind of like how you ran away from the Fish. But God had work for Jonah to do. In his mercy, God used the fish to bring Jonah back to Nineveh. And because of Jonah's preaching, the whole city repented and turned back to God.**

Discuss the following.

- *What do you think about Jonah running away from God?*
- *Why do you think God went to such lengths to get Jonah to come back?*
- *Explain whether you've ever tried to run away from God or something you thought God wanted you to do. What happened?*

Close in prayer, thanking God for the mercy and grace he shows to us.

TIP It may sound strange, but wrapping bathroom tissue around someone's eyes and head three or four times works just as well as a blindfold. It's more sanitary and can be quickly removed.

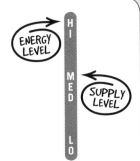

Best for

AGES 10-12

SCRIPTURE

Luke 1:26-38, 45

SUPPLIES

Bible, table, box of toothpicks, two rolls of masking tape

PREPARATION

On a table at one end of the room, set out half of the toothpicks. At the other end of the room, set out a roll of masking tape on the floor for each group.

Toothpick Relay

Broken toothpicks represent broken promises and help kids remember that God will always keep his promises to them.

Have kids count off by twos and have both groups line up at one end of the room.

Say: **Let's have a relay race. The first person in each line will hop to the table, break a toothpick in half, and hop back to the line. The next person in line will grab the tape, hop to the table, and tape the toothpick back together. Try to tape the toothpick back together exactly as it was before it was broken. When you are done taping the toothpick, hop back to the line carrying the tape. Then continue until everyone has either broken or taped together a toothpick. Ready? Go!**

When all of the toothpicks have been taped back together, have kids sit in a circle. Place the mended toothpicks in the center.

Debrief

Discuss the following.

- *Explain whether the toothpicks are as strong as they were before.*
- *How are mended toothpicks like broken promises?*
- *Tell about a time someone broke a promise to you.*

Read Luke 1:26-38, 45. Say: **In our race, it was hard to tape the tooth-picks back together exactly as they were before they were broken. Broken promises are hard to mend. That's why God keeps his promises. Mary knew that, and we can remember that, too.**

Jesus' Birth

AGES 10-12

The Waiting Game

This icebreaker helps kids discover that God delivers on his promises even when waiting is part of his plan.

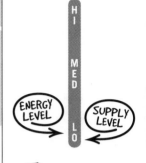

SCRIPTURE

Luke 2:25-33

SUPPLIES

Bible

PREPARATION

Ask kids how many days are left until Christmas.

Then say: **Most people think it's tough to wait for Christmas—and for other special events.**

Refer to Simeon in Luke 2:25-33, and talk about how he waited his entire life to meet baby Jesus!

Have kids form groups of three.

Say: **We're going to get to know one another better. Take turns introducing yourself to your group. Along with your name, tell the group about something special you're waiting for—or have waited for.**

Get kids started by introducing yourself. For example, you might say something such as, "Hi, I'm Mrs. Martinez, and I waited a long time for my trip to the Holy Land."

When the groups have finished, form one circle. Ask trios to take turns introducing their members to everyone. Start them off with a help-ful example, such as, "This is Johnny, and he waited a long time to go camping with his dad." Continue until everyone's introduced.

Debrief

Discuss the following questions.

- *Explain what it's like to wait for special days or events.*
- *Tell about a time you were frustrated or impatient—how did you act?*

Read aloud Luke 2:25-33. Then ask:

- *How did Simeon respond when he finally saw baby Jesus?*

Say: **God often makes us wait for the things we want, but he always delivers the things he promises.**

AGES 10-12

Feeding Fun

Kids have a food run to see how they can count on God to provide for them.

SCRIPTURE

Mark 6:30-44

SUPPLIES

Bible, furniture, bag of bagels, carton of fish crackers, rectangular laundry basket (the horizontal kind), napkins

PREPARATION

Arrange furniture or other objects to create a simple obstacle course. Place the bag of bagels and the carton of crackers in the laundry basket, and place the basket at the starting point of the course.

ALLERGY ALERT!
See page 8

Read aloud or briefly summarize about Jesus feeding the 5,000 in Mark 6:30-44. Have kids form groups of four. Explain that each group will get a turn to work together to balance the basket on their heads at the same time and move as one through the obstacle course. Each group will proceed through the course on its own while the other groups cheer them on.

Debrief

After the game, distribute napkins, crackers, and bagels to the kids. Let them discuss these questions in their groups:

- *Tell what you thought was easy about this game and what was difficult.*
- *Why do you think the disciples didn't just ask Jesus to do a miracle to feed people?*
- *How did this miracle show that Jesus cared for people?*
- *How does God show his care for you?*

Say: **We can always count on God. He knows exactly what we need, and he'll never let us down.**

AGES 10-12

Progressive Story

Kids complete a story based on an unfinished drawing.

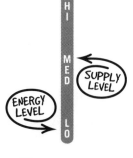

SCRIPTURE

John 20:1-18

SUPPLIES

Bible, additional adult volunteers, poster board or dry-erase board, marker

PREPARATION

Have kids form teams of three. Explain that all the teams will leave your room with an adult volunteer while you draw something.

Say: **One at a time, teams will come back into the room and will have three minutes to draw the next scene in a story. After each team has contributed its own scene using arrows to indicate the sequence of story parts, that team must leave the room again. No team is allowed to see other teams at work, but they will be able to see the scenes drawn ahead of them on the board.**

Instruct all the teams to leave the room, and then draw a simple version of a scene on poster board or a dry-erase board. Leave plenty of room for teams to draw. Try one of these scenes or your own idea:

• a person letting go of a bunch of balloons
• an elderly man bending down to pick up a $100 bill
• a couple of kids climbing a fence

When you're finished drawing, call in one team. Have that team draw the next scene and then leave, and so on.

When all the teams have drawn a scene, usher everyone back into the room. Have teams tell the story in sequence, with each team describing its scene. Then discuss the following.

• *What was it like to work separately but still finish our story?*

Say: **Just as you finished this story, God finished the story of salvation when he brought Jesus back to life. Everyone thought it was over when Jesus died. But God kept his promise and Jesus beat death!**

Close in prayer, thanking God for bringing Jesus back to life and finishing the story.

AGES 10-12

From Smirk to Smile

Kids explore some of the emotions Joseph's brothers experienced in reaction to his dreams.

SCRIPTURE

Genesis 37:1-11

SUPPLIES

Bible, timer or stopwatch

PREPARATION

With kids standing in a circle, choose someone to be the "Target" and another person to be the "Dream Teller." The Target's goal is to keep frowning while kids take turns being the Dream Teller and try to make him or her laugh using only their words and voices. Each Dream Teller will start a sentence by saying, "Listen to this dream I had. I dreamed that..." If after 30 seconds, or at the end of the sentence, the Target is not smiling, let another person try being the Dream Teller.

If the Target smiles, then the two trade places and the person standing to the right of the previous Dream Teller takes the next turn.

The game ends either when time runs out, or everyone has had a turn to be both a Dream Teller and the Target.

Debrief

After playing the game, have kids sit in a circle and discuss the following.

- *What was it like to try not to smile? to try to make someone else smile by telling a dream?*
- *Joseph's brothers weren't very happy about his dreams; how do you react when people tell you their dreams?*
- *Describe the most memorable dream you ever had.*
- *Joseph's brothers were angry and jealous of him and they didn't show love; how can you love your family even when you're angry with them?*

Best for

AGES 10-12

I've Got a Deal for You, Brother!

Kids explore what happened to Joseph and his brothers, learning that God works in all situations.

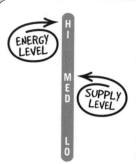

ENERGY LEVEL

HI MED LO

SUPPLY LEVEL

Give each person 10 candies (or marbles or beads) of varying colors, plus a plastic bag or envelope to hold them.

Say: **The goal of this game is to end up with 10 items of the same color by following these simple steps.**

1. **Each of you will decide how many items you want to trade, and hide those items in your hand.**
2. **You're allowed to trade up to three items at a time.**
3. **Begin to shout the number of items (up to three) you wish to trade. When you find someone shouting the same number, say, "I've got a deal for you, brother;" and make the trade.**
4. **You must give that person all of your trade items and take everything the other person is trading regardless of color. No picking and choosing.**
5. **Once you have 10 items of the same color, jump up and yell, "The market is closed!"**

Let kids practice to get the hang of the game before you play.

SCRIPTURE

Genesis 37:12-36

SUPPLIES

Bible; enough colored (wrapped) candies, beads, or marbles for every person to have 10; small plastic bag or envelope for each person (to hold the items)

PREPARATION

ALLERGY ALERT!
See page 8

After playing this game, discuss:

- *Joseph's brothers sold him to a caravan of traders.*
  Tell about a time you sold or traded something to another person.
- *Tell about a time you were really happy or regretted giving something
  to someone.*
- *What kinds of good things—if any—came from your experience?*
- *Ultimately, what good do you think came from what happened
  to Joseph?*

Say: **Joseph's brothers weren't very kind, but situations that start out
bad don't always end up that way. God can use the strangest, saddest
things for his purposes. He can turn those sad things around to show
his awesome power.**

AGES 10-12

Shoe Enough

Kids see what it's like to walk in
another person's shoes.

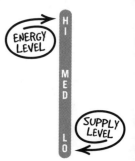

SCRIPTURE

Matthew 7:1-5;
Romans 15:7

SUPPLIES

Bible

PREPARATION

Form pairs and have partners remove their shoes. Tell partners to trade shoes, then stand against a wall. On "Go!" ask kids to each put their partner's shoes on the wrong feet and run to the end of the room and back. When kids return, they can trade shoes with their partner to get their own shoes back. Once everyone's own shoes are back on, they're finished.

Debrief

After the game, say: **A well-known saying is "Don't judge another person until you've walked a mile in his or her shoes."**

Ask:

- *Explain what you think that saying means.*
- *What was this game like for you?*

Read aloud Matthew 7:1-5. Ask:

- *What do you think it means to judge someone?*
- *Why do you think God doesn't want us to judge others?*
- *How can we "walk a mile" in someone else's shoes?*

Read aloud Romans 15:7, and close in prayer.

Best for

AGES 10-12

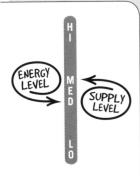

SCRIPTURE

Philippians 2:3-4;
Galatians 6:3

SUPPLIES

Bible, a timer or
stopwatch, 10 marbles
for each child

PREPARATION

Loving God, Serving You

Kids learn to focus on others rather than on themselves.

Give each child 10 marbles. Allow kids to mingle and talk about the previous week. Explain the catch: Nobody can say the word "I." Whenever someone says "I," any listener who hears it gets a marble from that person.

Count marbles after five minutes.

Debrief

At the end of the game, say: **It's hard not to talk about ourselves!** Read aloud Philippians 2:3-4.

Ask kids to discuss the following.

* *What was it like to talk to each other without using the word "I"?*
* *According to these verses, tell whether you think it's okay to talk about yourself.*
* *Why do you think God wants us to focus on others rather than ourselves?*
* *Tell about a friend you care about.*

Read aloud Galatians 6:3. Say: **This verse tells us to be humble and help others.** Ask:

* *How can we show others we care about them?*

AGES 10-12

Money Hunt

As they explore the widow's offering,
kids discover how to give to God.

With kids in groups of up to five kids, assign each group one of the colors of the fake bills. Explain to groups that they'll search for fake $100 bills of that color and collect all that they find. Also explain that the bill with the gold star is the most important one of all. When they find it, they have to return to you immediately and celebrate their great fortune!

Give groups five minutes to search (or more or less, depending on the size of your group and meeting area). When all the groups have returned, celebrate together. If any group wasn't able to find its gold-star bill, have the others join in to help find all the gold-star bills.

Then, ask the kids to give you all the bills they found, with emphasis on the gold-star bills.

Debrief

Afterward, ask kids to sit in their groups. Read aloud Mark 12:41-44, and discuss the following.

- *Explain what you were thinking when your team found the bill with the gold star.*
- *What did you think when I asked you to give me what you found, including the starred bill?*
- *In the Bible, why do you think the widow's offering was worth more than the rich people's offerings?*
- *What do you have to offer to God, even if you don't have a lot of money?*

Say: **God wants us to give from our hearts. Giving is good, but what matters more is that we give because we love God.**

SCRIPTURE

Mark 12:41-44

SUPPLIES

Bible; fake $100 bills (five of the same color for each group of up to five kids; use a different color for each group); gold star stickers (one per group); tape (optional)

PREPARATION

Before the game, place a gold star sticker on one bill of each color. Then hide and/or tape all the bills in "hiding" places around your meeting area, with the star bill hidden the best.

TIP If the fake bills don't come in colors, create your own by copying them on different colors of paper.

Best for

AGES 10-12

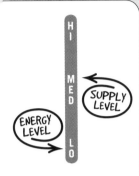

When You Grow Up

While pretending to have different careers, kids learn that God has a plan for us.

SCRIPTURE

Exodus 4:1-5

SUPPLIES

Bible, masking tape, permanent marker or pen

PREPARATION

Tear off a 3-inch piece of masking tape per child. On each piece, write a different occupation (for example: teacher, doctor, veterinarian, pastor, cook, and so on).

Read aloud Exodus 4:1-5. Say: **God had a plan for Moses to be a great leader, and God gave Moses everything he needed to follow God's plan. God has a plan for you, too.**

Encourage kids to share a time they had to plan to do something (be ready with your own example). Without letting kids see the word you wrote, stick a piece of tape onto each child's forehead (avoiding hair).

Say: **I just taped a pretend future job on your forehead. Now you'll walk around and ask only yes-or-no questions to figure out your job. Don't tell anyone any answers other than "yes" and "no."**

Allow about five minutes for kids to guess what's written on their foreheads.

Debrief

After the game, discuss the following.

- *Explain whether the job on your forehead is close at all to what you want to do when you grow up.*
- *If you had the choice to find out God's real plan for your life, tell whether you'd want to know—and why.*
- *Tell about a time someone asked you to do something, but you didn't think you could do it.*
- *How does knowing that God has a plan for your life give you confidence?*

Tell kids to take off their tape. Say: **God had a job for Moses, but Moses didn't think he could do it. Moses tried to convince God that he wouldn't be a good leader. But God had a plan for Moses. God has a plan for you and he'll help you do it, even if you don't think you can.**

AGES 10-12

Replicate It

Kids discover why it's important to listen to God.

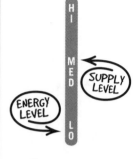

ENERGY LEVEL

SUPPLY LEVEL

HI MED LO

SCRIPTURE

Genesis 6:11-22

SUPPLIES

Bible, images of something easy to draw, markers, blank paper

PREPARATION

Say: **I'm going to pair each of you up and assign one person in each pair to be the "Instructor" and one to be the "Artist."**

Give the Instructors a picture of something a child could easily replicate and the Artists a blank sheet of paper and markers.

Say: **Sit back to back so you can't see each other's papers. When I say "Go!" the Instructors will tell the Artists what to draw and how to do it. The goal is for both pictures to look the same in the end without either partner seeing what the other has.**

Allow three to five minutes, then call time.

Debrief

After the game, discuss the following.

- *Explain whether you think this experience was easy or difficult.*
- *How was this game similar to how Noah built the ark?*
- *Explain whether you think it was important for the Artist to listen closely to the Instructor.*
- *What happens if we don't listen to God?*
- *What are ways we can listen more carefully to God?*

Read aloud Genesis 6:11-22. Say: **Just as the Artists had to listen carefully to the Instructors, Noah had to listen carefully to God. God knew what the ark should look like, and Noah had to listen and obey to create it. In the same way, God knows what our lives will look like. If we listen and obey him, he'll help us see how to live.**

AGES 10-12

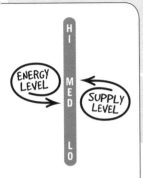

SCRIPTURE

Isaiah 49:1-3

SUPPLIES

Bible, paper, pencils, two sticky-hand novelty toys

PREPARATION

Snappin' Attributes

Kids "grab" papers with other kids' skills.

Say: **Let's play a game that'll help us learn more about the way God made us.**

Distribute paper and pencils, and direct kids to write on their papers in large, clear letters one skill or ability they have or wish they had.

Say: **You might write things such as, "ability to show kindness to others," "skill at playing basketball," or "ability to get good grades."**

Collect and shuffle the papers, and then scatter them on the floor around the room with the writing facing up. Then form two teams, and have the teams line up single file. Give the first person on each team a sticky hand.

Say: **The first person in line will use the sticky hand to "grab" one skill or ability from the floor and bring it back to your team. Then that person will give the sticky hand to the next person in line, who'll do the same thing. Your team's goal is to grab the skills or abilities that the team wants most, but you can't grab your own paper. Listen for your team's suggestions about which abilities to grab.**

When each team member has grabbed one paper, stop the game. Then allow teams to look over the skills and abilities they've collected and discuss whether they grabbed the abilities they wanted or not.

• Debrief • •

After the game, discuss:

- *How was this game like or unlike how you feel about the skills or abilities you've been given?*
- *Explain why you think we sometimes aren't satisfied with the skills and abilities we've been given.*

Read aloud Isaiah 49:1-3. Say: **What does this Scripture tell us about how God wants us to use the skills and abilities he has given us?**

Ask:

- *Why do you think it's important to be thankful for the skills and abilities God gives us?*

Say: **Unlike the prophet Isaiah, we may not understand why God has given us certain abilities. Sometimes we might not be satisfied with what we have. But even if we don't fully understand how to use our gifts and abilities for God's purposes, we can know that God helps us fulfill what he wants for our lives. He never stops thinking about us, and he's created a unique plan for each of us.**

Peer Pressure

AGES 10-12

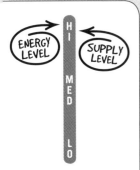

The Power of One

Kids learn that sometimes the right choice is not following the crowd.

SCRIPTURE

Romans 12:1-2

SUPPLIES

Bible; old bedsheet or blanket; small, soft balls (such as tennis balls) or beanbags; scissors; black permanent marker; name tags

PREPARATION

In the center of the sheet, cut a hole that's slightly larger than the diameter of the balls you're using. Number the balls and put corresponding numbers on the name tags and hand them out together. Spread the bed sheet on the floor.

 TIP If applicable, guide kids toward discussing any dangerous or immoral activities they may face, such as drinking alcohol, smoking tobacco, doing drugs, or stealing.

Give each person a numbered ball, and have everyone gather around the sheet. Then have kids place their numbered balls on the sheet. Next, have kids bend down and grab the edge of the sheet with both hands and on "Go!" begin pumping the sheet up and down. This action keeps the balls bouncing in the air and allows them to fall through the holes in the sheet, one at a time.

Play multiple rounds if time permits.

Debrief

After the game ends, ask kids to gather around.
Read aloud Romans 12:1-2, and say: **There's a lesson here. We all like to get along with our friends and do things together. However, in the ups and downs of life, there are times when it's important for us not to go along with the crowd. If we do, we might wind up like most of these balls did and just fall through the holes that are out there in the real world. There are times when the winner in real life is the one who doesn't go along with the crowd.**

Ask the group to discuss the following.

- *Describe some activities where you should avoid going along with the crowd.*
- *Tell about a time when you went along with the crowd or chose not to.*
- *What are some things you should never do, even if your friends really want to?*
- *Explain how you can say "no" and still be with your friends.*
- *Are there times when it would be best for you to find different friends who are more healthy influences?*

AGES 10-12

Stressed Out!

Kids see that God wants their lives
to be stress-free.

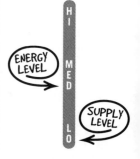

SCRIPTURE

Philippians 4:6

SUPPLIES

Bible, balloons

PREPARATION

BALLOON ALERT!
See page 8

Give each child a balloon to inflate and tie off. Ask kids to each place a balloon gently under one foot.

Say: **This balloon represents you and your foot represents stress that is not placed in God's hands. I'm going to call out things that can cause stress in your life. Maybe what I call out causes just a little stress for you. If so, put a little pressure on your balloon. Or perhaps it causes a lot of stress for you. If so, put a lot of pressure on your balloon. Don't release the pressure—just keep adding to it as I call out stressful things.**

Call out things that can cause stress in a child's life, such as fighting with a sibling, a test at school, a family move, being sick, a pet dying, too much to do, breaking a friend's electronic device, and so on.

Continue to call out stresses until you can't think of anything else or the balloons are all popped. Together, pick up all the balloon pieces and discard them.

Debrief

After the game, discuss the following.

- *What was this experience like for you?*
- *What was it like to press on your balloon?*
- *Describe what happens when you're stressed out.*

Read aloud Philippians 4:6. Ask:

- *In what ways can God help us with the stress in our lives?*

Say: **Let's do what God tells us to do when we're anxious or stressed. Let's pray for one another right now.**

Invite kids to find a partner to pray with, asking God to help each other overcome the stressful things in their lives.

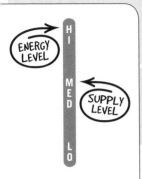

Best for

AGES 10-12

SUPPLIES

For each team, you'll need: a large jingle bell; a stick horse or broom; a cleaning tool other than a broom, such as a dust pan; laundry basket

PREPARATION

Giddyup Christmas

Kids enjoy this silly relay during the Christmas season.

Form teams of six or fewer, and have the teams line up at one end of the room with the props at the other end. Give the first person in each line a jingle bell to shake as he or she runs to the other end of the room and performs a series of activities. Once they've completed all the activities, have kids shake their bells as they return to their teams and pass the bells to the next people in line. Play until everyone's had a chance to do the activities.

Demonstrate the following activities and then say "Go!" for teams to begin.

1. **Donkey Ride**—Ride a stick horse or broom in a circle and say, "Giddyup, giddyup!" Lay down the "horse."

2. **The Inn**—Wave a cleaning tool (other than a broom) in the air, and say, "No 'broom' in the inn."

3. **Manger**—Sit in a laundry basket and say, "They laid him in a manger."

4. **Angel**—Flap your arms like wings and say, "Glory in the highest."

Debrief

Discuss the following questions together.

- *Explain what it was like to rush through this game.*
- *Why do some people forget what Christmas is all about?*
- *How can you help yourself remember the true meaning of Christmas?*

Say: **Each station in today's relay race made up a retelling of Jesus' birth, but if you were concentrating on winning the race, you might have missed that. There's a lot going on at Christmas and we can sometimes get distracted. This Christmas, let's take time to focus on Jesus.**

God's Love Is for YOU!

Permission to photocopy this handout from *The Giant Book of Games for Children's Ministry* granted for local church use.
Copyright © 2013 Group Publishing, Inc.,1515 Cascade Ave., Loveland, CO 80538. group.com

God's Love Is for YOU!

Permission to photocopy this handout from *The Giant Book of Games for Children's Ministry* granted for local church use.
Copyright © 2013 Group Publishing, Inc.,1515 Cascade Ave., Loveland, CO 80538. group.com

Indexes

Energy Level
....
Scripture
....
Topic
....
Supply Level

Energy Level Index

Medium Energy

High Energy

Upper Elementary Games

GIANT BOOK OF GAMES FOR CHILDREN'S MINISTRY

Scripture Index

Topic Index

GIANT BOOK OF GAMES FOR CHILDREN'S MINISTRY

Supply Level Index

Medium Supplies

High Supplies

Upper Elementary Games

Low Supplies

Medium Supplies

High Supplies

GIANT BOOK OF GAMES FOR CHILDREN'S MINISTRY

Great ideas from real experts!

100 BEST IDEAS to turbocharge your children's ministry

Dale Hudson & Scott Werner

Group

▶ ISBN 978-0-7644-9853-4 • $19.99

100 Best Ideas to Turbocharge Your Children's Ministry

Dale Hudson & Scott Werner

A treasure trove of tools and techniques to take your children's ministry to the next level...and impact kids' lives like never before. These 100 sure-fire "how-tos" were developed by children's ministry leaders who've spent years fine-tuning the strategies that bring real success. You'll discover how to:

- Equip volunteers to love serving and stay for the long haul
- Develop a dynamic ministry area that kids love and bring their friends to
- Rev up your vision and get your team excited
- And much, much more!

You'll be ready to fuel your children's ministry to do great things for God, for your church, and for you.

ALSO AVAILABLE:
100 Best Ideas to Turbocharge Your Preschool Ministry
▶ ISBN 978-0-7644-9852-7 • $19.99

Order today! Visit group.com or your favorite Christian retailer.

Group

Nearly 200 **BIBLE STORY CRAFTS** to choose from!

The Encyclopedia of
Bible Crafts
for Children

Kids love crafts! And teachers love to use crafts that connect with Bible stories. This hefty and handy volume offers approximately 200 craft options for nearly every major Bible story! Great add-on item for curriculum.

- 200 (give or take a few) field-tested crafts for every book of the Bible in one easy-to-use, jumbo volume! Proven to work and to delight children.

- Crafts will help children connect with Bible truths even more memorably.

- Handy indexes help you find just the right craft for the Bible story or Bible book you are teaching on.

▶ ISBN 978-0-7644-2395-6 • $29.99

Also Available:

The Encyclopedia of Bible Crafts for Preschoolers

▶ ISBN 978-0-7644-2621-6
$29.99

Order today! Visit group.com or your favorite Christian retailer.

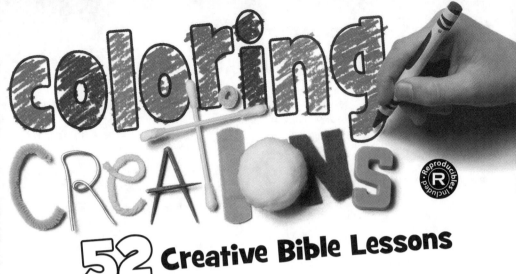

52 Creative Bible Lessons

Coloring Creations:

52 Bible Activity Pages

Use these reproducible coloring masters as fun time fillers that will expand the lesson of the day, and give children a conversation-starter to take home and share with the rest of the family.

More than just a coloring book— each coloring page is a 3-D, multi-sensory, super-tactile creation! Your kids will color the page, decorate it, cut it, fold it, paint it, and all around change it.

These 52 Bible activity pages include coloring fun that references Scripture from the Old and New Testaments:

- Jesus Gives the Disciples an Amazing Catch
- The Good Samaritan
- Jesus Changes Water Into Wine
- The Woman at the Well
- Jesus Is the Good Shepherd
- Jesus Washes the Disciples' Feet
- You Can Have a Friendship With Jesus
- God's Holy Spirit Is Like the Wind
- Church Brings Us All Together
- Paul and Silas Teach the Jailer That Everyone Can Know Jesus
- We Are Part of God's Family
- Care for One Another, and more!

Handy indexes organized by Scripture reference and Bible story name.

Coloring Creations
▶ ISBN 978-0-7644-2767-1 • $19.99

Coloring Creations 2
▶ ISBN 978-0-7644-3506-5 • $19.99

Order today! Visit group.com or your favorite Christian retailer.

Secret weapons for *getting kids' attention!*

Throw & Tell® Balls

Group's Throw & Tell Balls get—and keep—kids' attention when you finish a lesson early, kids show up grumpy, or you need an icebreaker—fast! Simply inflate a sturdy, colorful ball and let kids toss the ball around for a few seconds. When you call "Time," the child holding the ball reads what's written under his or her left thumb—and then everyone answers (or the child answers, depending on how you choose to play). Kids love the Throw & Tell Balls, and you'll love seeing them open up, laugh, and connect with one another in this new way.

NOTE: All balls inflate to 24" diameter. Comes in hangable bag.

THROW & TELL BALLS   *For age 3+ only*

[A] ATTENTION-GRABBER THROW & TELL BALL
for Children's Ministry
Perfect for grabbing kids' attention, then launching your lessons!
▶ UPC 646847-10995-9 • $9.99

[B] PRAYER THROW & TELL BALL
for Children's Ministry
53 prayer prompts help kids learn more about poverty.
▶ UPC 646847-12156-2 • $9.99

[C] ALL ABOUT ME THROW & TELL BALL
for Children's Ministry
Encourage kids to learn about each other and find common connections!
▶ UPC 646847-16933-5 • $9.99

[D] THIS...OR THAT? THROW & TELL BALL
for Preteen Ministry
Keep kids on the edge of their seats with this hilarious ball of fully loaded questions.
▶ UPC 646847-16934-2 • $9.99

[E] PRESCHOOL THROW & TELL BALL
for Preschool Ministry
It's fun. It's super-easy. It's bouncy. And it's GUARANTEED to get your preschoolers to open up and interact!
▶ ISBN 978-0-7644-7613-6 • $9.99

[F] LIFE-APPLICATION THROW & TELL BALL
for Children's Ministry
Dozens of instant application activities!
▶ UPC 646847-10988-1 • $9.99

Order today! Visit group.com
or your favorite Christian retailer.